creation: artistic
and spiritual

Translated from the French
Original title: CRÉATION ARTISTIQUE
ET CRÉATION SPIRITUELLE

Omraam Mikhaël Aïvanhov

Creation: Artistic and Spiritual

2nd edition
Second printing April 2000

Izvor Collection — No. 223

PROSVETA

Canadian Cataloguing in Publication Data

Aïvanhov, Omraam Mikhaël, 1900-1986
    Creation : artistic and spiritual

    (Izvor collection ; 223A)
    2nd ed., 2nd print. Apr. 2000
    Translation of: Création artistique et création spirituelle.
    ISBN 1-895978-21-1

    1. Creation (Literary, artistic, etc.) 2. Spirituality. I. Title.
II. Series: Izvor collection (North Hatley, Quebec) ; 223A.

BH301.C84A3513 2000   128'.3   C00-900473-4

Prosveta Inc.
3950, Albert Mines, North Hatley, QC, Canada J0B 2C0

TABLE OF CONTENTS

1

ART, SCIENCE AND RELIGION

If we want to have a really clear idea of this question of art, we have to take as our starting point the structure of man himself.

A human being can be defined as a trinity: he has been given a mind with which to think, a heart with which to feel, and a will with which to act. The goal of the mind is science, knowledge; the specific concern of the heart is religion and ethics, whereas the will is designed for action: it needs to do something, to build and create. This is why we can say that art concerns the will. Music, dancing, sculpture, architecture, poetry, painting and so on, are all means that man has invented in order to express outwardly, in concrete form, what is in his heart and mind. Art, therefore, is related both to science and to religion.

Science requires light; religion warmth, and art creative activity. Unfortunately, human beings have the habit of separating science, art and religion into three separate compartments;

in fact they often consider them to be mutually contradictory. One finds frequent instances in which religion has condemned science and art, in which science has scorned religion and considered art to be too trivial to be taken seriously, or in which art has set little store by the opinion that either science or religion may have of it! And yet, in life and in nature, the three are closely linked: they work together. Initiates have never separated the three domains. But now that men have separated them, religion no longer has a hold on scientists: they reject it out of hand. In point of fact, of course, if scientists reject religion it is because they do not possess true science. They are only interested in the physical, material world, not in the science of the three worlds which is the only true science, and on which all religions are based. As for art, it hovers uncertainly between the two: at times it is at odds with religion and morality and, at other times, with science.

In nature, as I have said, religion, science and art are one. It is only in the minds of human beings that they have become divorced, and as long as this state of separation persists there can be no true understanding of reality. Science, religion and art together form a coherent whole which enables us to explain and understand the whole of creation. In man, the activity of the heart, mind and will must never be set one against the other. All three must move in the same direction, united and inseparable: when the intellect judges that something is good, the heart must contribute all its strength, love and enthusiasm and the will must ratify the judgment of the heart by acting upon it. If the intellect disapproves and condemns what the heart feels as good, or if the will is torn first one way and then the other in the attempt to satisfy their conflicting commands, it will be thrown completely off balance, and man will disintegrate. The intellect needs science, the heart needs religion and the will needs art; it needs to express itself, to create and build. And these three needs are intimately related, for the thoughts of your mind are felt and loved by the heart and, eventually, translated into action by the will.

What does life show us? It shows us that man begins by planning things in his mind; next he feels the desire to see his plans carried out and, finally, he sets to work to put that desire into effect. You see: thought, feeling and action. Thought must always precede action. Of course, people very often do just the opposite: they act before they have studied a question properly, and the results are frequently disastrous and cause them untold suffering and remorse. One might ask, 'Is it ever permissible to act without thinking?' Yes, it is, but only if one is so pure and so

highly evolved that every impulse to act comes as
a direct inspiration from God Himself. There are
a few, extremely rare and exceptional beings who
are so intimately identified with the Godhead
that if they paused to reflect before acting they
would be allowing a human element to intervene,
and this would disturb the divine energies which
have exclusive control of them. Once they have
acted, beings such as this can look at what they
have done and see that it is good, just as God
Himself saw that what He had created was good.
If you study the story of the six days of creation in
Genesis, you will see that each 'day' God spoke a
few words which brought the different elements
of the universe into existence and that, at the end
of each day, He looked at what He had created
and 'saw that it was good.' If we want to do as God
does, we must be like Him — and if we want to be
like Him we are going to have to work hard for
several billion more years!

Turn and turn about, science, religion and
art have each thrust themselves into first place in
the different civilizations of the world at different
periods of history. For a very long time it was
religion which predominated in the West, hinder-
ing the development of art and science. Then
came a period in which religion declined and
science gained the upper hand. And now one can
say that the future belongs to the artists. Yes,

more and more we see that people appreciate and applaud art and artists; Heaven has chosen, at this moment in history, to manifest itself through artists, musicians, poets, painters and sculptors. What is the reason for this?

Nothing is more necessary to man than art. It is something which goes back to the infancy of mankind itself. And, in fact, can one not see this in the first manifestations of a human baby? He does not bother his head with philosophy, science or morals; he is an 'artist': he spends his time gesticulating, screwing up his face and screaming. Malicious gossip might say he is crying, but I must object: No, he is singing — or, at least, let's say that he is exercising his lungs and vocal chords against the day when they will be fully formed and ready to sing! Then look at how he dances, just as soon as he can stand on his own two feet; and how he draws and paints, even before he has learned to read or write! Give him some building blocks or some sand, and you will see the budding architect at work.

The history of mankind was marked, first of all, by art. Later, religion assumed first place and, finally, science predominated. But in future, I repeat: art will be predominant. 'Why art?' you may ask: 'Why not religion or science?'

For centuries, religion — or rather those who have represented the religions — have been

unworthy of their mission and have neglected
their spiritual goals for other, material goals:
authority, prestige, power and money. Instead of
instilling true faith into the hearts of men, they
have taught them fanaticism; instead of freeing
them, they have all too often tried to subjugate
and exploit them. Jesus castigated the scribes and
Pharisees, saying: 'Woe to you, scribes and
Pharisees, hypocrites! For you shut up the kingdom of heaven against men; for you neither go in
yourselves, nor do you allow those who are enter-
ing to go in', and his rebuke could be applied with
equal justice to most of the clergy of the world's
religions. This is why more and more people are
abandoning the churches and temples. As for
science, all its energies are spent on such highly
specialized research that it has become the affair
of experts only. Even if they recognize the utility
of scientific discoveries, most people cannot
really understand them or make them their centre
of interest.

Only art has the power, nowadays, to touch
men profoundly and awaken them to the true life.
This does not mean that no criticism can be made
of the forms assumed by art today, on the contrary; in fact it would be true to say that it is very,
very far from the ideal of art as the Initiates
understand it: an activity in which both true
science and true religion are united. And yet, it is

art that will save the world, an art that is conscious and enlightened by the truths of wisdom
and love. In the future, artists will rank first in
human society, for a true artist is priest,
philosopher and scientist. Yes, for the function of
an artist is to carry out on the physical plane that
which intelligence conceives as truth and the
heart feels as good, in order to permit the world
above, the world of the Spirit, to descend and
become incarnate in matter.

2

THE DIVINE SOURCES OF INSPIRATION

Man will never improve anything on this earth if he does not begin by raising his mind to higher levels so as to contemplate other images, other modes of existence superior to his own, and find his models and guidelines in them.

Jesus said, 'Thy will be done on earth as it is in Heaven.' He could not have expressed such a prayer if he had not already contemplated Heaven and seen that everything there was so perfect, so glorious, that one could not help wishing that the earth would, one day, be like that. But this implies, necessarily, that man must be capable of rising above the shabby, mediocre, fragmented realities of this earth in order to contemplate the realities of Heaven and, having contemplated them, of returning to organize and adjust earthly realities to conform to the models he has seen on high. And this is the work of Initiates: through their meditations and contemplations they perceive and tune in to the perfection of the world above, which they then endeavour to reproduce here, on earth. But it is only in Initiatic schools that human beings learn to do this: most men have no idea how to rise to a higher plane, above and beyond that of the earth, so as to contemplate that higher world, and this is why they have made such a ghastly mess of this world below.

The only purpose of meditation and contemplation is to enable man to reach a higher plane of consciousness which will influence and colour his tastes, judgments and attitudes. The problem is, though, that one must know how to meditate, how to contemplate, and what subjects to choose. A great many people meditate, but they meditate about the most prosaic things: how to organize their businesses, how to earn more money, how to steal a kiss from a lovely woman! You ask somebody, 'What are you doing?' 'I'm meditating!' But only the Lord knows what he's meditating about! A cat meditates, too: it meditates on the problem of how to catch a mouse. So, you see, there are different kinds of meditation. And since, in spite of all their meditations, human beings are still bogged down in the same old faults and failings, the same perversions and infamy, it is obvious that they have not yet grasped the secret of true meditation.

True meditation is, first and foremost, to

raise one's mind to a world far superior to one's own little world, to lose oneself in wonder and admiration of it and, then, to reflect that wonder in oneself. If you still feel cold, dingy and uninspired after your meditation it means that it was a failure. Meditation should change something in the way you look, in your smile, your gestures, the way you move; it should give you something new, something subtler: just one little particle, perhaps, but a particle that vibrates in harmony with the divine world. This is how you can tell whether you have meditated well or not.

When you meditate, begin by choosing a very elevated subject on which to fix your mind. After a few moments you can relax your mental concentration and simply contemplate and soak yourself in the beauty you have conjured up in your mind's eye. And finally, if you are able, you can identify with that beauty. The first step, therefore, is concentration, followed by meditation, and then, once the ground is prepared, comes the stage of contemplation: you pause to bask, as it were, in the image of perfection that fills your heart and mind, to drink deeply of its beauty, to savour it and find happiness in it. And, finally, you identify with it — and this is plenitude.

There! Now you know some very useful methods (they are more than useful, in fact: they are magnificent!), and if you apply them you should be able to draw great benefits from your meditations. Otherwise you will fritter your life away, deluding yourself into believing that you have achieved something worthwhile, whereas in reality you have accomplished nothing.

The great geniuses of the past; painters, sculptors, musicians and poets, applied these methods, and that is how they were able to bequeath their masterpieces to humanity.

Before starting work they recollected themselves and meditated and prayed for Heavenly blessings, for only Heaven can give us the light which illuminates the imagination. The result of this approach was that they received the revelation of true beauty and were enabled to express and communicate it to others. If a man is capable of producing great works of art when he is acting under inspiration, it is because all his faculties work together in harmony with the spiritual light received from above. No immortal work of art can ever be produced without inspiration from the spirit.

It is striking to see how many ancient poets began their poems with an invocation to the gods or muses. This was an acknowledgement of the fact that, before an artist begins to create, he must turn to beings of a higher order and ask them to collaborate in his work. The soul and spirit of man possess antennae by means of which he can communicate with the Almighty. God created man in His own image and, consequently, gave him the power to create great marvels, but this power needs to be cultivated and cared for, and not despised and neglected as is the case in most instances today.

Where will you find artists who pray and meditate before beginning work, today? They are all geniuses, you understand! They don't need any help from Heaven; they don't need to be inspired! And this is why the element of eternity which gave works of art of the past such inestimable value, is absent from the work of contemporary artists. And not only that, but it mainly reflects the infernal, subterranean layers of the subconscious. The artists who create works of this kind are leading mankind to destruction. And the same must be said of thinkers and writers who have never meditated or experienced ecstasy, who have never risen to celestial heights or contemplated the structure of the universe: they write books which have a destructive, disintegrating effect on their readers by filling them with doubt and revolt and a taste for disorder and anarchy. A great many of the books published today are written by authors who have never made the effort to raise themselves to the higher regions of the spirit. Perhaps you will ask, 'How

can you know that?' The answer is not compli-
cated: I know it simply by seeing what effect their
works produce in human beings. If a writer fails
to awaken our higher nature it is a sure sign that
he has never visited the Heavenly heights.

When you contemplate the masterpieces of
an artist who has been genuinely inspired by
Heaven, you are in contact with the beings of a
higher order who inspired him, and you begin to
sense and experience something of the artist's
own experience; you are almost forced, whether
you like it or not, to tread the path he trod: he
takes you by the hand and leads you into the
regions that he has explored and contemplated.
And this is why art is useful: this is the educational value of art. When a man rises to higher
spheres he absorbs particles from those regions
which continue to be active and vibrate within
him; in fact they vibrate in such a way as to operate
all kinds of transformations in the world. This is
the ideal of a true artist, the ideal of an Initiate.

In short, Initiates, mystics and artists resem-
ble each other in that they all have a favourable
influence on mankind: artists, through their
works of art; mystics, through their spiritual
emotions and virtues, and Initiates and the great
Masters (whom I rank above all others because
they are in almost direct contact with Heaven)
through their capacity to spread light. Artists

work to produce forms which adhere as closely as possible to the ideal of perfect beauty; mystics and religious men and women work to improve the psychic and moral dimension, that is to say that they work on the level of content, whereas Initiates and the great Masters work on the level of meaning, on ideas and principles. These three categories of beings are united in their desire ceaselessly to improve and perfect humanity, but they go about it in different ways in keeping with their different capacities and talents: artists on the level of form, mystics on the level of content and Initiates on the level of meaning. Artists, mystics and Initiates all have different faculties, different means of expression and different missions. But the reality, the quintessence, is one and the same; only the expression is different.

These three categories of human beings correspond to the three essential principles in man: spirit, soul and body; intellect, heart and will; thought, feeling and action. All three are essential, but the priority goes to intelligence and understanding; ethics, mysticism and a generous, sensitive heart come second, and action, the work of making the world a better place, comes third. A whole man is one who is capable of embracing all three worlds: philosophy, religion (including ethics) and art.

The foremost desire of a true Initiate is to work for the accomplishment of Jesus' prayer: ' Thy will be done on earth as it is in heaven'. This prayer contains the whole of Initiatic philosophy, the whole plan of action for a disciple, a true Christian. It is no good just reciting the words and hoping that the Lord will send someone else to accomplish it in actuality: no! It is up to us to do it; it is our job to set to work and make the earth like Heaven.

But there is one thing you have to realize, and that is that if you are not willing to spend enough time, effort and love to raise yourself to the heights so as to contemplate and comprehend the realities of Heaven, you will never bring Heaven down to earth in any form whatsoever. For these things cannot be done just anyhow. It is not possible to express beauty without first learning how to communicate with beauty. And yet there are a great many artists who think that even though they live shallow, shoddy lives, they are going to create sublime works of art. No, as long as they do nothing to bring order into their lives and to purify themselves they will simply produce objects of horror: accurate expressions of their own degree of evolution!

Besides, man is only man; he cannot express divine, eternal beauty in all its purity. As the pure reality passes through him, through his heart and mind, it is tainted by elements of his own human nature and individual temperament. The degree of beauty to which an artist can attain, therefore, and which he can express in his work, depends enormously on what kind of person he is. Beauty is like a beam of light, it can only be seen in all its brightness if you look at it through a perfectly transparent medium. If your medium is tinted, dirty or opaque, the light will appear to be deflected and deformed. This is why it is so important that an artist should have done a great deal of work on himself before he starts to create: he must become a medium so vibrant and transparent that divine beauty will not be deformed as it passes through him.

I am sure you know the saying, 'The prettiest girl in the world can only give what she's got!' Obviously, if you want to give, you must first possess. And isn't it even more obvious, that if you want to create, you must possess the elements of that creation within you? If someone shows you a monstrously ugly work that he has produced, it means that he has monsters of ugliness within him; there is no need to look any further. No one can produce divine works of art if he is not inhabited by Heavenly beings; in order to produce something greater than oneself, one has to transcend one's own limitations and journey to higher regions, and there gather divine elements which may then be communicated to others. This, then, is the secret of divine art : to transcend oneself in order to give mankind something better.

People are always looking for something better, something new and more beautiful. This is what they are looking for when they go to theatres and cinemas, concerts, libraries, exhibitions and museums : something better. Every human being has this deep instinct within him to seek something better, but the poor wretches don't know that instead of looking for it in concert halls, theatres, music-halls or night-clubs they should rise to the higher levels of the soul and spirit where they would find inspiration.

What is inspiration? It is an entity which enters a human being, takes possession of him and expresses itself through him. It will perhaps help you to understand this better if you take the case of a pianist or violinist who gives frequent concerts. Some evenings his playing is nothing out of the ordinary, no one is particularly moved by it ; nothing emanates or radiates from him, no special force flows from him to move his audience and transport them to sublime heights. On other occasions, all at once, something seems to enter into him, and without his realizing it — but that 'something' which has entered him realizes it perfectly — his touch, his movements and even

the way he holds himself in relation to his instrument, are all different, and something inexplica-
ble happens. Then his audience is deeply moved
and they say, 'It was simply wonderful, divine!
He's inspired!'

Esoteric Science teaches that inspiration is
simply a contact, a communication with a force,
an intelligence, an entity belonging to a higher
level of reality, which uses us to achieve something that we could never achieve on our own. A
poet, for instance, may want to compose a poem:
he sits there with a blank piece of paper in front of
him and nothing comes. He feels utterly sterile:
no inspiration. And then, all of a sudden, something seems to enter into him, a light, a current,
and he abandons himself to it: he does not even
have to hunt for words, they come to him as
though they were being dictated, and he is the
first to be astonished by what he writes. Where
did it all come from? What entity is capable of
finding all those materials and elements and
combining them to create expressive forms of
such beauty?

Left to his own devices, a human being is not
capable of creating superhuman, divine works of
genius, but he may be visited and inspired by very
highly evolved entities. This is why he must learn
how to attract such entities. They are waiting all
around us, and they are so overjoyed when they

see a human being who has learned to introduce
light, order and peace into his existence, that they
hasten to enter into him to help him and others
through him.

Cosmic Intelligence has ensured that the
human race shall continue to evolve and progress
by giving men the instinct to move constantly for-
ward, to open up new horizons. Look at the plant
and animal kingdoms: they are still the same
after thousands of years, their evolution is very
slow, whereas human beings are capable of
advancing very rapidly. The trouble is, though,
that if men are not guided and taught by Initiates
and Masters, they are so fascinated by the external, objective, superficial aspect of life that they
fall victim to it and become enslaved. They are
always looking for greater satisfaction outside
themselves, always expecting to find greater joy
on the fringes of reality, in human creations. But
they will not find it there: to find what they are
looking for they have to look upwards — or down
into their own depths, if you prefer; it is just a
different way of expressing the same reality.
Whatever wonders man has succeeded in creating, they are no more than a pale, distant reflection of the divine world.

Even the very greatest artists are limited in
their means of expression; they can never tran-

scribe exactly what they see, hear or feel in their moments of inspiration. Even Beethoven, Mozart, Leonardo da Vinci, Michelangelo or Rembrandt were unable to communicate all that they saw and heard. So you must not think that the best way to hasten your evolution is to visit museums and art galleries. Of course, I am not saying you should not do so; on the contrary, it can certainly be useful. For my part I have visited museums and art galleries, temples and churches, and attended concerts and plays in every country I have been to; but that is nothing, really nothing, compared to my excursions into other regions. It is in those other regions that I have learned and grasped and contemplated splendours which surpass all the masterpieces of this world. That is why, when I am shown certain 'creations' I cannot feel any special respect or admiration. It is not my fault: I have been shown things which are so much more beautiful and more perfect!

So now, since you have seen for yourselves that the advice and methods I have given you over the years have always been true, useful and full of good sense, I ask you to listen attentively to the advice I am giving you today and to surpass and transcend yourselves in order to become true creators.

3

THE WORK OF THE IMAGINATION

Everybody dreams, wishes and imagines; and since everybody imagines, everybody thinks that they know what the imagination is. But they are mistaken: the imagination, such as the Initiates conceive it, can be described as a kind of screen which lies at the frontier between the visible and the invisible worlds, and on this screen are projected images and entities not normally within our field of consciousness. The imagination of certain very highly evolved human beings who know how to use this faculty, receives and records a great many impressions which they then attempt to express or describe and realize. When they do this, their contemporaries may not understand what those realizations correspond to, but later they see that they reflect a perception of realities which already existed but which had not previously been manifested on the physical plane. If a man knows how to model and govern his own thoughts and feelings, he becomes capable of purifying his psyche to such an extent that his imagination becomes transparent and crystal-clear, and he begins to 'see' the things of the subtle worlds. At this level, imagination and vision are one.

But the aspect I wish to talk about today is that of the formative power of the imagination. The imagination is like a pregnant woman: as soon as she receives the living germ she sets to work to fashion and bring into the world a child whose character and physical and psychological nature correspond to the nature of that germ. Like a woman, the imagination moulds and nurtures the elements it receives; its power is formative rather than creative. Thought creates and the imagination forms. This is just one more instance of the way in which the two principles, masculine and feminine, can be seen at work: the masculine principle, represented by thought, acting on the feminine principle, represented by the imagination.

Thought is represented by the sun and imagination by the moon, symbol of all that is changeable and unstable. If the imagination is allowed to roam at large, if it is not harnessed to some useful task by an intelligent will, it soon becomes no better than a prostitute. For this reason a disciple must not allow his 'wife', his imagination, to dally in places of disrepute, for she will bring monsters home in her womb. He must give her clear-cut, luminous ideas and images so that she can work at moulding and shaping them into concrete form. This is how a disciple becomes a magus. A magus is one who is capable of impregnating his imagination, his faithful and devoted spouse, with an idea or desire which he has, himself, created and prepared at length and in detail, secure in the knowledge that she will carry it out for him.

It is time that human beings became aware of the faculties the Creator has placed in them so as to cultivate and exploit them to the full, instead of neglecting them and allowing them to run wild for, one day, they will be turned against them. Hospitals and asylums are full of people who have never learned to control their imaginations, and amongst them are a great many so-called artists who thought that artistic creativity consisted in allowing a free rein to their imagination. No, indeed! You have to control your imagination.

Sometimes you can feel that you are inhabited by a beneficial influence, and at these times your imagination forms splendid images. But at other times, if you are not very vigilant, if you are not always fully conscious, entities of darkness can insinuate their pernicious seed into you, and then your imagination gives birth to deformed, diseased 'children'. You may well be unaware of it, but this is something that happens quite frequently. Some of you will perhaps say, 'But I haven't got any children!' Others will say, 'I have two or three children and they're all perfectly normal!' Well, if they only knew it, they have hundreds of sick, deformed, half-witted children clinging to them in the form of inner turmoil, psychoses and obsessions which play havoc with their lives. What can you expect? 'Like father like son'!

The power of the imagination is tremendous, and if you so rarely get any sensational results with it, it is because you have not persevered faithfully in the good work you started: you have been undermining your own work by your contradictory behaviour. Suppose, for instance, that you have been trying to make your physical features more harmonious: if you do not learn, first of all, to master your inner impulses and the chaotic desires which continue to occupy your imagination, they will continue to deform your features. The concrete realization of your most divine dreams demands a lot of conscious, intelligent, organized work. And if you don't see any results in this incarnation, don't be discouraged: you will see them in the next. Perhaps you will ask, 'Why can't I get results in this incarnation?' The answer is that in your previous incarnation, you gave your 'wife' some specific tasks which she carried out to the letter, and the result is what you are today. And now, if you want to change that, you will need time: a lot of time. If, in the past, you had had an instructor and the will to work you would have seen much better results today. In any case, however that may be, make up your minds here and now to do the work that must be done, otherwise, in your next incarnation, you will still be weak, ugly, ill and impoverished.

Your imagination works with the raw materials you give it; your thoughts and feelings, and if those thoughts and feelings are neither pure nor rational nor harmonious, is there any wonder if you now find yourself physically and psychologically impaired? Whose fault is that? Was it not you who formed your own body? Perhaps you will object that it was not you but your parents, and of course this does seem to be the case, because there always has to be a culprit on the physical plane. But the truth is that the real culprit is you yourself. I have often heard people say, 'Nobody asked me if I wanted to be born! My father was a drunkard, my mother was a prostitute; they spent their time quarrelling and fighting and they thrashed me unmercifully! They never gave me enough to eat or enough clothes to wear; I had no money to buy books for school. Is there any wonder that I don't amount to much now? It's all my parents' fault.' And, of course, everyone will agree with him: 'It's not his fault, poor fellow. If only he'd had a good family background, etc., etc.' Yes, but why did he incarnate in a family like that? Was it mere chance? No, it was not! The Science in the name of which I am speaking tells us that absolute Justice and Intelligence do exist, and that they are responsible for the conditions in which each human being reincarnates; the family, the country and the point in time, and that this decision corresponds exactly to what each person deserves. I assure you, I have studied all this and can vouch for it.

But even if we cannot change what we are to any great extent here and now, that is no reason to be discouraged and perpetually miserable. God has given human beings the capacity to correct their mistakes and change themselves. Even if you have great difficulty, at the moment, in actually achieving what you want to achieve, keep working at it with your imagination, and don't try to put a time limit on it: in the long run it will all come about. For our imagination has the power to attract elements which correspond to the thoughts and feelings with which we nourish it. Wherever those elements may be, at the bottom of the ocean or high in the heavens, it knows how to find them and store them up and, one fine day, we shall be surprised and delighted to find that our ideas have been given shape and material substance. Yes, the imagination is so powerful it can shape even our physical bodies.

The imagination, like a woman, works in accordance with the great laws of creation, but this does not mean that we can leave it to its own resources: it needs to be controlled and guided. Young people who are ignorant of human nature (and it is no use counting on their schools to enlighten them!), have no idea how dangerous it is to let their imagination run riot, for it is perfectly capable of turning into a confirmed harlot! Even educators allow the young to remain in a hazy, dreamy state of mind; in fact they encourage them to do so: 'He lives in his dream world; he's a poet, let him dream!' Yes, but do they know what the world of dreams is like? Do they know what true poetry is? Nature has endowed men with considerable powers which must be used for good, and if young people allow their imagination to become a prey to every passing feeling or desire they will end by being invaded and completely dominated by very negative forces.

So you must study this tremendous question of the imagination and know that if you let it wander without restraint or guidance, you will fall a victim to evil influences; they will take control of you and leave you completely off-balance and defenceless. An Initiate does not allow his 'wife' to flirt with all and sundry. He is permanently in control, and he has a care to fertilize her divinely so that she may give birth to wonderful, beautiful children: light, kindness, justice and truth.

Unfortunately, most people use their imagination to satisfy their basest desires: seduce a woman, injure an enemy, get rid of a competitor — they do all this in their imagination. And, perhaps, one day, their dreams will come true; but what good will that do, even to them? Why not use one's imagination to resuscitate, build up one's own strength and capacities and achieve something divine for the whole of humanity? Why not imagine that all over the world, men and women become good, intelligent, honest and beautiful, and that joy and plenty reign everywhere? If you work for years, picturing only bright, positive things in your imagination, they will end by coming true; and if hundreds and thousands of people worked in the same direction they would come true even sooner. But it is difficult to get human beings to unite for this purpose; there are always some who destroy what others build: in these conditions nothing good can be accomplished, even the best ideas are bound to be stillborn. This is why we must all unite and work together.

I told you a moment ago that the imagination is related to the moon. When the moon is waxing one's imagination tends to run along much more positive lines than when the moon is on the wane. During the waning of the moon, our minds are more vulnerable to the impressions of negative images, and those who have not already trained themselves and worked in the psychic dimension, put up no resistance and allow themselves to be overrun. If you watch your own reactions you will see that this is so.

Lead your imagination into heavenly places and let it contemplate those worlds of beauty, so that it may then reflect them. The imagination is a messenger: you can send it far, far away to register and bring back to you the splendours of Heaven itself. Many painters, poets and musicians have found inspiration in this manner. Instead of looking for it in low, unwholesome company, as most artists are in the habit of doing today, they travelled mentally to the sublime regions above where they captured visions and impressions which they then attempted to translate into paintings, poetry and music.

The imagination can be compared to the sounding balloons which meteorologists send up to record and send back to earth information about atmospheric conditions and prevailing winds and currents. But, as I say, one can best compare the imagination to a woman, a woman who has the power to bring into the world exactly the child that you ask her for: and this is where the vital role of the will becomes evident. You only have to say, ' I want a child with eyes and hair of such and such a colour, with a body like this and a voice like that... ', and your imagination will give it to you.

I have no doubt that my way of presenting things astonishes you. You would not hear unacademic explanations like mine in a university ! But most people understand and remember simple, concrete explanations full of imagery and I want to be understood by as many people as possible.

Now that you know these great magic truths of Esoteric Science you must review your lives and turn a spotlight on your present shortcomings. Are you an absolute dunce where science or the arts are concerned ? Have you never developed the qualities of the heart ? Have you never tried to be kind, generous and magnanimous ? Are you a weakling, an 'ugly duckling', with neither physical beauty nor strength ? Do you lack stamina and good health ? Even if all that is true it does not matter ; don't be discouraged. As

long as you are still alive you can give your imagination the germs of all the qualities and virtues
you need, and in your next incarnation you will
see results. In fact, even in this one, you will find
that something in you changes.

No desire, whether good or bad, remains
unfulfilled. As soon as you formulate a desire in
your own heart it becomes a reality on a subtler
level. But it takes a long time, years perhaps, or
even centuries, for it to become a visible, tangible
reality on the physical level. But if you have the
patience to concentrate on one idea until your
imagination condenses it, it will really and truly
become a concrete, visible reality.

Be careful, though: since all desires end by
becoming reality, if you allow yourself to wish for
things which are not reasonable you will be very
unhappy when they come true, and however
much you try to escape from them, by then it will
be too late. You will have to put up with the suffering they cause you, and wait for death to put an
end to what you yourself, in your ignorance, had
created.

On the other hand, if you do not see the fulfilment of your good desires, don't lose heart,
don't be unhappy; go on believing and working.
Isn't it really marvellous to know that, one day,
you will achieve all you hope for? But you must
hope only for what is best and most useful for the

whole world. To want to be a musician, poet, physicist or Minister is not bad — but it is not the best ! The best thing we can possibly ask for is to be so transformed that we may bring light, warmth and life to all creatures : there is nothing better than that.

4

PROSE AND POETRY

Poetry often seems to be a world of nebulous, incoherent images, which may be very beautiful perhaps, but which have nothing in common with the language of Nature. Those who are responsible for this false conception of poetry are the poets themselves who haunt the lower astral planes and fall a prey to the seductions of the entities who make their homes there. This is why the masses who have no criteria by which to judge and who are, anyway, very inclined to live in a confused, misty state of consciousness, are enchanted by the poetry they produce, and follow them blindfold into the darkness of those regions. I assure you! I have seen how people understand poetry.

All too often, also, the first thing poets do is to pour out all their most negative feelings, all their sorrow, disappointment and despair into their poetry. Why do they have to feed the public on their pain and revolt? It is as though they were giving them excrement to eat. And people are so stupid they accept it all: it almost seems as though they felt the need to regale themselves day and night on refuse and offal. Oh, I know that what I am saying is so foreign to your own conceptions that it is not easy for you to understand. But you will gradually acquire more adequate criteria by which to judge art, and then you will no longer admire certain works or types of art that can only bring on an attack of colic, migraine or eczema — on the spiritual level! Too much of what passes for art today is simply the projection of a very inferior, foolish mentality.

What is true poetry, then? True poetry is the divine Word in which all the elements are marvellously interlinked by secret bonds of correspondence. True poetry awakens in man memories of his heavenly fatherland; it sets the most highly spiritual cords of his being vibrating, it gives him the impetus to create the new life. And this is why, if a poem gives you only a few vague flutters of sensation and fails to arouse any deeper emotional response, you can be sure that it is not true poetry.

When I was very young, I was full of enthusiasm for poetry. In fact I composed mystical verses and tales into which I wove many spiritual truths, visions and prophecies. But I stopped writing poetry as soon as I realized that it was debilitating: I found that it made me hyper-sensitive and vulnerable and tied me to the astral, lunar regions. So I abandoned those regions and went to look for true poetry in the sun. And now, if you feel that there is poetry in some of the explanations I give you, it is because I have trans-posed that poetry into the areas of science and philosophy. True poetry is to be found in nature, for in nature everything is both beautiful and scientific. Nowadays we are in the habit of divorc-ing science from poetry, but in nature they are one.

Poetry must be based on a higher learning, a divine understanding; if it is not, it is worthless and can even do harm. This is why Plato, who possessed true Initiatic Science, said that there was no room for poets in his Ideal City (because poetry, as it is commonly understood, is a world of illusion and falsehood, a dim reflection of true poetry), whereas philosophers and scientists were welcome.

Personally, I love poetry; in fact I rank it higher than music, painting, sculpture and so on. Poetry is the divine Word, the Logos. And the Logos is music, colour, form and perfume all at the same time. To be sure, music is a very powerful medium, the effect it produces on the listener is direct and immediate. But the language of music is not as clear and instructive as the language of poetry. The clarity of the Logos comes from the use of words, for words enable us not only to see forms, colours and dimensions but also to hear a melody, a rhythm and an intonation. And, above all, they enable us to perceive meaning.

Music arouses feelings and stimulates the will but it does not give any clear indication of direction. You can listen to music your whole life long and still be as ignorant in the end as you were in the beginning! Whereas if you listen to poetry, not only are your feelings aroused but also, thanks to the words used, you can reflect on its meaning and find direction in it. And besides, there is music in it too, as well as colour, form and architecture! All the arts are contained in poetry. Many people feel that music is the art form which surpasses all the others, and if you take into account only the power and intensity of its action, this is perfectly true: music seizes and captivates; it takes one prisoner as it were. Whereas when one listens to poetry one's understanding also has to come into play, so that, although it does also captivate one, it requires more mental activity.

The fact is that true poetry is not confined to the field of literature, it is part of life. The true poet is he who is capable of *living* the poetry expressed in his verses, who is capable of living, thinking, feeling and acting poetically. It is all too easy to compose poetry whilst continuing to live a very unpoetic life! Many poets are incapable of writing anything without the stimulus of alcohol, tobacco and endless love affairs! Apparently they need all these different experiences and the sensations they get from them in order to prevent the 'springs' of inspiration from running dry. But the springs of these sorry poets ran dry a long time ago! And now they are sick and vulnerable, totally lacking in will-power, exposed to every passing breeze, perpetually in the grip of passions and torments, slaves to their own excesses — and they end their lives in insanity or the gutter!

I have known a great many poets in my life and have had ample opportunity to study them at close quarters. I do not deny that they are often very gifted and very sensitive; some of them have real genius. But they have not developed their inner strengths; they have no will-power, no balance, and they think that in order to be creative they have to plunge into the depths of the underworld. What a brilliant idea! To be sure, if you don't live to the full, if your life is not rich in experiences, you cannot create: that is true. But why go and look for your materials down below, in the subconscious and the sordid substrata of life? You will, of course, find material there, but it will not be the best kind. Why not look for experiences in other areas and become acquainted, for instance, with heaven, purity and divine love?

I am all for experiences, but they must be celestial, not infernal experiences. All the great geniuses of the past had celestial experiences with the result that they were capable of creating masterpieces, whereas the majority of artists today delight in immersing themselves in filth. And once they are thoroughly steeped in it, they write about it, on the pretext that one must depict human nature 'as it really is'. But they don't know human nature; all they know is the inferior, infernal part of man, and this is what they serve up to the public. In the future, poets will, once again, sing of purity and intelligence, of the beauty of God and of the universe. They will nourish men with the dew from Heaven and divine Ambrosia, and the world will live in true poetry.

At the moment, if one is the least little bit observant, one is forced to admit that the lives of even the most highly cultivated and most learned human beings are totally unpoetical; they are cold and wooden; there is no warmth, no spark of fire in them. This is what I call 'prose'. Why is mankind turning more and more to prose? Poetry has become something that only concerns the poets who write it. From time to time, of course, people will read a few lines of poetry, but

their lives are not poetic. And this is why I say that
the new art, the art of the future, will consist in
learning to live every minute of the day and night
poetically, by which I mean to be vibrantly alive,
warm and expressive! Only when you are like that
will others begin to love you. Human beings just
don't understand: their one desire is to be loved,
but who wants to love a block of ice? They are
cold, lifeless and unresponsive: prosaic, in fact!
They have no idea how to live the kind of poetic
life that would endear them to others.

When I greet you in the morning and look at
all your faces, I can see that some of you live in
poetry: they are glowing with love and light, they
give something, whereas the others look cold and
congealed; they have not learned the new art of
giving and radiating. How can anyone teach them
this? Even when they have an example before
their eyes they remain frozen in their prose: stiff,
unreceptive, hostile and thoroughly disagreeable.
If they were intelligent they would understand
that this attitude can never be to their advantage,
that it is time to adopt another attitude, to begin
to live in poetry, for poetry is life, true life.

Evolution is an ascent towards the Godhead.
And this being so, why cannot people understand
that if they are always dingy and lack-lustre,
frozen and congealed it means that they are going
in the opposite direction, they are sliding back

towards the mineral reign, they are becoming stones? When people adopt this attitude they are unaware that life will use its sledge-hammers to break up this stone and use it to build something new. That is the inevitable fate of stone, and the only way to avoid the danger is to come alive again. If you want to go back to being a stone no one is going to stop you, but you will be broken. On the other hand, if you become alive and vibrant, in the first place you will have a much better chance of avoiding being broken and, secondly, you will be in a position to help others, even those who are far away, just as the sun helps all creatures by sending its rays of light and life into space.

Make a practice of sharing something of your own light and warmth every day. Believe me, it is an excellent exercise and it will help you to go out from yourself a little, to free yourself from a terribly stagnant, prosaic situation. Here, in the Brotherhood, you will learn to live constantly in a poetic state of mind. Surely you know how delightful it is to meet a poet, someone in whom one can sense that everything is vibrantly alive and radiant with light? When I meet someone like that I am quite incapable of concealing the joy it gives me; my whole being expands and I feel like throwing my arms round him and hugging him! A human face that radiates signals of light is very contagious. Unfortunately, all those harmful elements which thrive in men and women have paralysed them; even when they try, they are incapable of showing an open, smiling countenance, they remain aloof and unsmiling. Their facial muscles refuse to cooperate, they are totally wooden and expressionless, and when they do attempt a smile they only manage a twisted grimace. When I see someone who finds it difficult to smile at people and look at them with love, I realize that the poor fellow has spent his whole life stagnating in the lower regions of his will, heart and mind, and that he has never had the joy of being visited by an element of the soul or the spirit. When the soul and spirit burst onto the scene they change everything: nothing is more beautiful than the manifestations of the soul and spirit, nothing lovelier than their radiance, their emanations.

People are taught only one thing in the world: to take, always to take. But here you are going to have to learn to give, which means to look at others with love, to smile, to squeeze out of your heart a few little particles to give to others. If you do this you will feel something expanding inside you; you will be amazed at how happy you feel. Human beings are always afraid of losing something, of being deprived; they don't understand that this fearful, grudging attitude is the very thing that impoverishes them. If you want to be rich you have to give.

When you take you become poorer; when you give you become richer. Indeed this is so, because giving triggers unsuspected forces which have been stagnating in the depths of one's being; as soon as one wants to share them they begin to circulate and flow more and more abundantly and one is astonished to feel so enriched. People exclaim, 'But what happens? How can you explain it? I have given and given and yet I am richer now than I was before!' Well, that is the way it is: that is the new life. In the old way of life one takes and takes, and the more one takes the more one feels deprived and mean. Try to understand what I am saying; it is very simple. This is a new point of view, a new and absolutely true philosophy which you can test and prove for yourselves; in fact you have already proved the truth of it to yourselves time and time again, for you have all done something kind for someone and felt happy about it. On the other hand, when you have wounded someone and been unkind, you have felt miserable for the rest of the day. True, some people are proud of themselves when they have been rude to someone, but that is not the case for the disciples in an Initiatic School!

But let's get back to poetry. You will certainly find that my definition of poetry and prose are unlike any other you have ever heard. Yes, poetry is all that is alive, vibrant, mobile, all that is changeable and elusive. Sentimental temperaments have an affinity for poetry, whereas intellectual temperaments are more attracted by prose. This is because when the intellect wants to work and manifest itself it has to pin down and immobilize whatever it is studying. Why do you suppose that materialistic science has neglected the study of what is alive, and concentrated on what is dead? It is because the spiritual and divine worlds are alive with vibrations of such intensity that they are beyond the reach of scientific investigation. Scientists, therefore, are obliged to restrict their observations to the purely material, and this is why I say they are prosaic. If human beings are unhappy it is often because they attach more importance to the physical, material dimension; money, houses, land, etc., and all that contains little in the way of life. It is time, now, to pay far more attention to all that is alive and vibrant. In this way you will enter the poetic reality of the divine world.

Look at a child: he never stops moving, in other words he lives in the world of poetry! Later, when he is a young man, adults will tell him: 'Listen, you mustn't be so idealistic. Why on earth did you have to fall in love with a girl from a working-class family? Don't be an idiot! You know very well that So-and-so would marry you like a shot — and her father's a banker! You have to think of your career. Think of your future!' Yes, young people are carefully coached in the ways of prose: how to look out for 'number one', how to calculate all the advantages of any situation. And the result is that the poor young idealist ends by giving in and becomes just like everybody else: immobile, expressionless and prosaic, whereas before, he was expressive, vibrant and alive — he was a poet! So that is what it is to be a poet: to be always in motion. There you have a philosophical explanation of a phenomenon which you can witness with your own eyes every day.

Human beings are not in the habit of attaching much importance to occupations which could restore them to life. Look, for instance, at the question of prayer, meditation and contemplation, all those activities which can make a man's existence so extraordinarily poetic, and release inner forces capable of neutralizing the poison of any negative conditions he may suffer from: they are all neglected. People prefer prose. Look around you and you will see for yourselves that this is true for nine tenths of humanity. Haven't we had enough of all these prosaic people? For my part I want to have nothing to do with them! Being with people like that is like being in a freezer: they are so cold you have to wrap yourself in fur coats. The day will come when the most grotesque and laughable thing in the world will be the spectacle of an ignorant fellow who thinks that his frigid, haughty attitude marks him out as being a cut above everyone else! Actually, though, prehistoric animals like that will not exist any longer, or if they do they will all be at the zoo. Yes, there will be special zoos for extinct species like that!

Henceforth, therefore, think about introducing poetry into your lives. I say 'poetry', but I could just as well say 'the spiritual life' as opposed to the purely material life. In fact, whatever terms you use it all boils down to the two notions: spirit and matter. In itself, of course, there is nothing wrong with prose; there is nothing intrinsically bad about it. We all use prose when we write, and it can say a great deal, perhaps more, even, than poetry. But in poetry there is that intangible, indefinable element which uplifts and enchants. Prose speaks to the intellect: it enables you to understand ideas and notions, to describe, classify and explain, and all that is admirable. We must not discard all prose for it is indispensable, and there are a great many prosaic things in life which one simply has to do — I don't need to enumerate them for you. But we must not restrict ourselves to those things; if we do, they will deaden our sensibilities and numb us, and that is a form of impoverishment. So we have to find and treasure that poetic element which puts us in touch with Heaven.

Young people love poetry and music, for music always goes hand in hand with poetry. They are two expressions of the same region of the soul and spirit. Where there is music you will always find poetry too. And the fact that the young have this taste for poetry is a sign that they are capable of rising to much subtler regions. It is true, of course, that the songs, music and poetry they like are far from the best, but the mere fact that they do have a taste for poetry and music is a good sign. The only thing is that they need to be guided and instructed; they need to know that modern poetry and music — like all the art forms today, actually — are so dreadfully prosaic because the divine elements which make for true music, poetry and art, have gone out of them.

Only our higher nature can furnish the elements we need if we are to expand our consciousness to infinite horizons. And we must not forget that it is tremendously profitable for us to possess those elements: it is even better for our health; far better. If you rob a human being of all the poetry in his life, what is left to him? A purely vegetable life: he will eat and sleep and work, to be sure, but he will lack that intense inner vibration that stimulates and gives him his capacity for wonderment. Little by little, in fact, you would see that even his physical functions would slow down, and toxic wastes which should normally be eliminated, would begin to accumulate and form deposits in his organism.

So, if only for the sake of one's health, this kind of slow-motion life is not to be recommended. Of course, most people do recommend it because they think that it is the only 'sensible' way of living, and they criticize the poetic life with its wonders and ecstasies in the belief that it is a manifestation of something that is not quite sane! Many adolescents who had a leaning towards the poetic life, who might have flowered in this way, have been so scoffed and jeered at that, little by little, they have conformed to the standards of their environment and have become just as prosaic, just as 'wooden' as everyone else. And this is how people annihilate the best tendencies in the young, unaware that in stifling the life that stimulates and heals, they are stifling the power of the spirit which permeates all our cells, purifying them and giving them vibrancy; unaware, in other words, that they are introducing death into those young people. You may object, 'But you can't always go about looking as though you were in ecstasy?' Of course not! That is not what I am saying: you must not abandon all sense of proportion. In fact, if it happens at some point that you simply cannot contain your joy, you would do well to go and hide and do your laughing or crying in private, and wait until you have calmed down again before appearing in public in a 'normal' state of mind!

The Gospel tells us that only those who become like little children will be allowed into the Kingdom of Heaven. So be careful about your expression, for children are always laughing and smiling, and if you arrive at the gates of Heaven with a long face, they will tell you, 'No admittance for you! There is no light in your face, you are too dingy and gloomy. We can't have someone with a gloomy face like that in Heaven. We only accept those who have a childlike expression.' It is true you know: there are guards before the gates of Heaven to inspect the faces of newcomers, and if your face is not up to the mark they will turn you away, saying, 'Go away. Go back where you came from; here we live in poetry and

we want nothing to do with such a prosaic face!'
Well — if you don't believe me, you had better just
go and see for yourselves!

5

THE HUMAN VOICE

When I first arrived in Paris in 1937, I often went to concerts, the opera or plays, and I used to take advantage of these occasions to analyse the effect of different types of human voice on myself and the other people in the audience, and as I possessed the criteria for this analysis, I found it to be a very enriching experience. It is very interesting to know which centres in our organism are set in motion in response to certain sounds. This is an area of science which has remained virtually unexplored, and musicians, conductors, sound engineers, teachers and doctors would do well to apply themselves to a serious study of it, for there is a wealth of information waiting to be discovered here.

When one reads the Bible story of how Joshua and his people threw down the walls of Jericho with the sound of their trumpets, or the myth of Orpheus who used his lyre to charm, not only human beings, but also wild animals, rocks, stormy seas and even Cerberus, the watch-dog of Hades, it is clear that, from earliest antiquity, Initiates have known that sounds can have a magical influence not only on living beings but also on matter.

When I was at a concert or at the opera I used to close my eyes so that I could more easily study the effect of the singers' voices on my different centres, and the manner in which the vibrations communicated themselves and aroused this or that faculty.

Some voices are gentle and inspire peace, others excite violence. Some are so crystal-clear that the listener is bathed in a flood of purity and light, whereas others cast a cloud of darkness over the listener or arouse his sensuality. Some voices encourage reason, others madness. Some incite one to love, others to hatred. Some arouse one to action, others paralyse one... and so on. The examples are endless and it would take hours to enumerate them, but to put it all in a nutshell let me say that there are three main categories of the human voice: those which act on the will, stimulating or numbing it; those which enlighten or cloud the mind, and those which arouse lofty sentiments or, on the contrary, kindle vulgar passions.

In the past, musicians have been more interested in instruments than in the human voice: the voice is a domain which has been left largely unexplored. They have a tendency to think that the voice is less expressive than an instrument, but this is quite untrue. In fact the history of vocal music contains a great many singers of such immense talent that legends have grown up around them: singers such as Caruso, Chaliapine, Adelina Patti or Melba. There is a story that, one day, when Adelina Patti was on tour, she went to cash a cheque at the bank but she had forgotten to take any identification with her and the cashier refused to give her her money, so Patti began to sing! Her singing was so beautiful, so sublime that, of course, everyone instantly recognized her and she got her money! So you see what power a human voice can have: it can open doors, even the doors of a safe!

If the human voice has not yet revealed its true wealth or manifested the full range of its powers, it is because singers are not careful enough about the way they live. Unlike other, external musical instruments, the vocal cords are not independent of their owner. All that the person experiences in his life, therefore, including all the thoughts and feelings that go through his mind and heart, have repercussions on the voice. If a singer indulges in certain faults or failings, however marvellous his technique, these faults and failings will transpire in the quality of his voice.

Singers who are truly interested in cultivating their voice and want to be sure to keep it in good condition for a long time, must not only take great care of their health, they must also keep a close watch on their emotions. Even the slightest emotion, be it anxiety or fear, doubt, anger, joy or hope, will be reflected in the voice. Why do you suppose that, when you are in the grip of violent anger or fear, you are incapable of producing a sound? Whereas, when you are in love you feel moved to sing aloud! It is love that has the power to create a beautiful voice. So, if you want to sing beautifully you will have to fall in love with someone or something, and my advice to you is to fall in love with something — it makes everything much simpler! Fall in love with something tremendously elevated which will never cause you any problems and always be an inspiration to you!

When a singer lives a pure, well-balanced, harmonious life and maintains close contact with nature, his voice becomes stronger and increases in volume, flexibility and agility; it becomes sweeter and subtler and more obedient to his will so that he has greater control over it and can give truer expression to every shade of feeling. Instead of using it to flatter his own vanity or achieve the satisfaction of his passions and his appetite for pleasure and financial gain, he must use it to soar upwards, towards a high ideal. In doing so he forges bonds of friendship with the perfect beings of the spiritual world, who then help him and guide him along his path, and provide him with more and more possibilities for working and improving his voice. To be sure, this is not an easy path, but the sacrifices it demands are well worth it.

There are altogether too many singers, both male and female, who use their voices to communicate inharmonious and unhealthy vibrations to their audience, and in doing so they thrust them back towards a state of chaos, perversity and passion. Where are those who use their voices to inspire in their audience the desire to abandon their dingy, mediocre lives and start a new kind of life, dedicated to beauty and light ?

What we need today are singers who are also magicians; singers capable of using their voices to shake people out of their lethargy. But only those who have worked for years and years to increase the breadth, intensity and purity of their aura are capable of having such an effect on the souls of men. Yes, it is the artist's aura which creates the conditions needed for his singing to have a magical effect on his audience.

When Heaven gives someone a lovely voice, it is giving them something of great value which will enable them to perform miracles. The trouble is that they don't know how to use it and, above all, they are not sufficiently convinced of its worth. Singers are often spoilt children who do not realize what a treasure they have received and, especially, who have never thought about how they should use it. They need to work for and to achieve an ideal. An artist's ideal must be to lead people back to the Fountainhead; if he does this his name will be inscribed in the Book of Life: it will go down on record that he has saved many souls from tribulation and death. And he need have no fears for his own soul: if he saves other souls, someone else will come and save his! When someone scatters joy all around him, others come to give him even more joy.

When artists of this calibre have to answer critics or members of their audience who want to know how they acquired such a magnificent voice, what training they had, what special discipline they had to submit to, and so on; instead of expounding all kinds of futile theories or talking exclusively about their careers, they will answer in such a way as to enlighten other human beings and reinforce their desire to transform themselves. They will explain that the human soul is a daughter of God, and that if one wants to know it in all its glory one has to live a godly life. An artist can never have any really profound influence on the souls of his audience if he himself has not already worked to develop the gifts and talents received from his Creator. One cannot move others if one gives voice only to what is mediocre and imperfect in oneself. And if we want to transform ourselves and become capable of giving voice to our soul, we have to embrace the teaching of an Initiatic school, for that is where we find enlightenment about every area of existence: nutrition, breathing, gestures and movements, feelings, thoughts, etc.

Singers must dedicate their talents to awakening souls to the light. Perhaps what I am about to say will seem hopelessly outdated to you, but why shouldn't singers refuse to perform for the rich and powerful — who are ready to pay for very expensive seats at a concert, no doubt, but who are not necessarily the most luminous of souls — and give free recitals for souls who are ready and willing to receive a divine impetus and to work for the new life? Why shouldn't they bring together all those who need some celestial nourishment and sing for them? They would probably earn less this way, but does that matter so much? Any creation born of a disinterested idea and used for the service of an impersonal cause, possesses the germ of immortality. He who is aware of this law is in a position to acquire true wealth, for the one achievement that is above all others is to win a soul for the light.

If you have received a beautiful voice, do you

imagine that it is only for your own benefit? No, you have been given it so that you can use it to do something for others. Sooner or later Heaven will ask you to account for the use you have made of this gift. If you are obliged to admit that you used it to become rich and famous, to entertain the rich and pander to their whims and wishes, to hold them captive in their own sensuality and passions, Heaven will simply take the gift away from you.

Singers who are conscious of having a role to play in awakening souls must learn how to work mentally on their vocal cords. Here is an exercise you can do: picture yourself standing in front of an immense crowd of people; you are surrounded by an aureole of radiant light; thousands are listening enraptured as you sing, deeply moved by the powerful, subtle energies flowing through the channel of your voice into their souls. Their hearts are opened, their intellects are bathed in light, and their wills are moved to decide that, henceforth, they will work only for good. Keep doing this exercise for months and years, and the day will come when your voice will awaken only the higher, divine nature of those who hear you.

6

CHORAL SINGING

Four part choral singing is an act of great significance.

In the first place it is a symbol of what we have to do to attune ourselves and harmonize with each other. The blending of voices over our heads is, at the same time, a blending of our souls and spirits.

Secondly, choral singing is an expression of our desire to embrace the universe, to be attuned to and in harmony with the whole. This is why, before you begin to sing, you should turn your attention inwards for a moment to still any agitation and put aside the concerns of everyday life so as to be in harmony with all creatures in the cosmos and capable of singing in unison with them.

And finally, the practice of singing in four parts is already a reflection, an expression on the physical plane, of the effort we have to make every day, several times a day, in fact, to bring our spirit, soul, mind and heart into a harmonious unity.

You could say that the four voices: bass, tenor, contralto and soprano, correspond to the four strings of a violin, for the violin is also a symbol of man. The G-string represents the heart, the D the intellect, the A the soul and the E the spirit. The violin itself represents the physical body, and the bow represents the will which plays on the four principles — heart, mind, soul and spirit.

The harmonious blending of the four voices, or the play on the four strings, is a reminder to us that the four principles: heart, mind, soul and spirit, must vibrate harmoniously within man. Why do you suppose that a violinist has to keep tuning his violin? Isn't it to teach us that we cannot make any genuine inner progress if all the parts of our being are not harmoniously tuned? More important than anything else, therefore, is to look into ourselves and be sure, before we do anything, that the 'strings of our violin' are correctly tuned.

It is very important to sing. To be sure, you can listen to records at home, as most people do. There are not many people in France who actually sing; it seems that they don't even feel the need to do so. And yet there is a tremendous difference between singing and listening to someone else singing. The difference is exactly the

same as that between eating and watching someone else eat ! If you are content to watch someone
else eat, it is he who will get fat and strong, and
you will wilt away. When he has finished his meal
he will be full of energy and ready to work,
whereas you will barely be able to move your little
finger. Yes, it is as different as that ! He who sings
puts himself in contact with the world of music,
whereas those who never sing become inwardly
weaker and weaker from lack of nourishment.
Music, and particularly singing, are a form of
nourishment which enables us to work on the
spiritual level. You will, perhaps, be surprised to
learn that while you are singing you are, at the
same time, doing some serious work, but it is so ;
on condition, of course, that you do not consider
singing simply as a pastime, but as an activity
which affects every aspect of your being.

If you study the Sephirotic Tree of Life, you
will see that music is an attribute of the Sephira
Chokmah in which reign the Cherubim. The
Cherubim are pure music, and they dwell, therefore, in perfect harmony. Chokmah is the region
of the Logos by Whom all things were created,
and the Logos is pure music, the harmonious
sounds that fashioned the universe. For sound
models matter and gives it form, and it was in this
way that, through the Logos, God fashioned the
formless, primeval matter, that which Genesis

terms the *thohu wa-bhohu*. God breathed His Word over that cosmic dust and forms appeared. Under the influence of the Logos, the Cherubim received a divine vibration, which was communicated thence to all creatures below the level of Chokmah, all the way down to Earth.

The Cherubim do nothing but sing together in harmony, and when human beings also try to sing in harmony they create a bond between themselves and the angelic Order of the Cherubim, the Order of music and Heavenly harmony. When you sing, therefore, whether you know it or not, you are establishing contact with the Cherubim and, in this way, the harmony of sounds works its effects on you; it causes the material particles of your body to vibrate in such a way that its physical forms will, one day, be a reflection of perfect beauty and harmony.

You can understand, therefore, that singing gives us the conditions most conducive to the purification and embellishment of our physical bodies. And one day your souls will begin to put out antennae capable of receiving cosmic energies from the region of Chokmah: you will feel yourselves inspired, you will hear the Music of the Spheres, you will sing with the choirs of Angels, and Wisdom will make its dwelling within you. Yes, for music is an expression of Wisdom: the Hebrew word 'Chokmah' means wisdom. Chokmah lies outside the range of our octave, it stretches beyond our solar system to embrace the Zodiac. And as the Zodiac symbolizes Immensity, the Cosmos, the Infinite, music transports us to such heights that we melt into that Immensity.

You really must try to understand all this and not be content to enjoy only the pleasurable sensations singing procures, for the beneficial effects of music reach far beyond sensation to the most sublime regions. If you really understand the question fully, I am confident that you will devote much more time to singing together, because you will begin to feel tangible results from it. You are perpetually engaged in activities which may seem to be of the first importance, but which are incapable of making you happier, nobler, healthier or more luminous ! The best they can do is to give you more material comforts and an easier life, but that contributes nothing to your transformation. Whereas when you sing together with real conviction, you are striving to attune yourselves to another, higher order of things and this transforms you and furthers your evolution.

And, you know, you can do this even when you are by yourself : if you feel lonely, unhappy or troubled in any way, pick out a song you would like to sing, put yourself in mental contact with the region of the Cherubim, and picture yourself singing with all the brothers and sisters throughout the world, and you will experience an influx of strength and inspiration. When you have been singing, even if you did not do so with the idea of obtaining any special results, you will find that life seems more beautiful, other creatures seem more agreeable and your will has a new firmness to it: so why not do this consciously?

You do not realize what a tremendous variety of means and materials you have at your disposal, so you don't make use of them, and this is the worst possible thing: to possess such riches and still feel wretched because you are not even aware that you possess them. If you devote more time to singing, therefore, and if each one of you without exception learns to sing in harmony, the results will be extraordinary. Singing is an invaluable instrument with which to work, firstly, on yourselves and, secondly, on the world around you, for the harmony that is in you reflects on your surroundings and, sooner or later, the whole world will experience its influence. Isn't this a wonderful way of working for the good of humanity?

All that we do in life is magic, but this is a fact that is widely ignored and misunderstood because people are afraid of the word 'magic'; they think it is something to be avoided and, as they don't study it or even recognize its existence, they have very mistaken notions about it. And yet all works of art: painting, sculpture and dance, and even the beauty of created things is magic! 'Magic' simply means influence, the effect or influence that one thing has on another. If, therefore, something exerts a beneficial influence on its surroundings, if it spreads peace, light and harmony, we say that it is white magic, divine magic. If, on the other hand, something has a disquieting influence and brings darkness and disorder in its train, we say that it is black, diabolical magic. It is important that you understand this and that you think, feel and act more and more constructively, positively and harmoniously. In this way you will become white magicians.

When you come together to sing, therefore, you wield tremendous magical power for good, but you must never forget that all power is based on unity and harmony. Remember that you must form a family. Leave aside all consideration of your different characters and tendencies, all the differences in your degree of evolution, social background or profession; forget about all that, for none of it really matters; none of it makes much difference in the spiritual life. Strengthen the conviction in your hearts that you all belong to the Universal White Brotherhood, and that you, as members of this Brotherhood, are singing together in order to awaken consciences throughout the world; if you do this then, indeed, you will be truly powerful.

Believe me, it is your unity that is the source of your power. Even if you don't like each other, therefore, even if you have had differences of opinion, none of that matters; get together to sing and you will work miracles. Perhaps you are thinking, 'Ah, if I see So-and-so I'll wring his neck for him!' That's fine, but first of all go and sing, and we'll see about the rest later! Start by singing, and it could be that once you have sung you will no longer be so set on wringing anyone's neck! You may not understand how you have become so tolerant, all of a sudden, but it is due to the singing which has already transformed you just a little and made you just a little gentler. So, whether you love or hate each other, whether you agree or disagree, it makes no difference: what matters is to achieve unity.

Do you imagine that soldiers who go to war together all get on well with each other simply because they are in the same regiment? Before being in the army they might well have been neighbours who detested each other cordially, but once they are united in common cause against an enemy, it is amazing what they are capable of doing together! They support and help each other, and even save each other's lives. And then, when the war is over, they probably begin quarrelling again; but at least they have proved that they are capable of working together for a time! And why should we be incapable of doing as much? In fact, I am convinced that, while you are singing and praying together, your misunderstandings are not just brushed aside for a time; they dissolve and disappear entirely, and you end by being incapable of quarrelling again. So that is the difference.

And now, how can you acquire this new awareness and become welded together and united by the work we are doing here? The accord that reigns amongst you must grow and be strengthened, for it is here, in the collectivity, that you will find true beauty and harmony. So instead of traipsing about all over the place, you would do much better to come here and sing, for that is the best way of setting in motion the work of purification, illumination and liberation that, without your even being aware of it, will restore order within you. In this way you will be preparing a nucleus, a cell of the new life for the benefit of all those who come here in the future. They will be staggered to see that, while they were still wasting their time and amusing themselves, you have been hard at work preparing for the coming of the new culture!

7

HOW TO LISTEN TO MUSIC

Everything in nature sings and vibrates; all creatures emit vibrations which are diffused around them in the form of musical waves. This is why it is true to say that everything in nature is music. There is music in a rushing stream, in the murmur of a spring, in the patter of raindrops, in the roar of a cataract and the ceaseless ebb and flow of the waves of the ocean. There is music in the voice of the wind, in the rustling of leaves and the twittering of birds. And the music of nature constantly arouses and stimulates the musical sentiment in man, kindling in him the desire to express himself through the medium of a musical instrument or through song. When man feels the need to communicate his feelings and emotions it is to music that he turns most spontaneously; when he wants to express his deepest religious sentiments he turns to music; all his joys and sorrows, his love and every profound experience is expressed in music.

Music is the breathing of man's soul and consciousness. It is through music that the soul manifests itself in the world. When man's higher consciousness is awakened, when he develops his capacity to perceive the subtler realities, he will begin to hear the great and glorious symphony that reverberates throughout space from one end of the universe to the other, and he will comprehend the deepest meaning of life.

Music awakens in our souls memories of the heavenly home from which we came and a yearning for that lost paradise. It is one of the most powerful mediums, far more powerful than painting or dance because it is so immediate, so instantaneous. In a flash one remembers that one has come from Heaven and that it is to Heaven that one must, one day, return. There are, to be sure, certain kinds of music which, on the contrary, arouse the desire to remain on earth as long as possible, but that is not the true function that music was intended to fill.

Everybody listens to music, but in an Initiatic school one learns to listen to music with a specific purpose in mind: to awaken one's spiritual chakras, to take flight into space and raise oneself to greater, nobler heights, to purify oneself and even to solve certain problems. When we listen to a piece of music we must, first of all, know what it represents, whether it is a force for good or for ill, and what it conveys to us: is it like the wind or like thunder? Is it like a cataract or a waterfall tumbling down the mountainside? Is it like electricity? Or heat? Whatever the energy it emits you must learn to use it. If it conveys the wind to you, you can imagine that you are on a ship in full sail. If it conveys electricity, you can use it to set your spiritual 'appliances' in motion, and so on. Music is a force. Each sound, each vibration triggers a movement in space and releases certain forces in man.

If we listen to music every day, after meals, it is because I want you to learn to use it creatively to accomplish something substantial in the way of spiritual work by projecting sublime ideas and imaginative pictures which will, one day, become concrete reality. Music can help you, especially mystical, deeply religious music which takes you out of yourself and transports you to great heights.

Many intensely spiritual people have scorned the help that music could have given them in their work, and they were wrong to do so. Music can be an extremely powerful means by which to awaken dormant cells, to achieve a higher degree of nobility and to transform and perfect oneself: one should not ignore it.

Let others think and live as they please, but you, who are seeking to advance in the spiritual life, must learn to make use of everything that God has given you. A disciple is someone who is determined to use his time and energy and all the materials that nature and the Lord have given him in order to achieve or earn something more. He is like the servant in the Gospels who invested the few talents his master had given him before leaving for a long journey, so that they would earn more, rather than burying them away where they would be unproductive. A disciple is an intelligent, sensible servant; he uses everything that Heaven has put at his disposal to accomplish a divine task: whether it be air, water, or food, whether it be his thoughts and feelings, or his own body, his eyes and his ears or all the innumerable things that exist in nature; he learns how to put all these things to good use. He learns how to get everything working for him and he becomes more prosperous, day by day, whilst others waste their time frittering away their energies and beggaring themselves for want of effective methods and the right notions about how to work.

While you listen to music, therefore, work with it, use it to form all the things you wish for in your mind. You want so many things and yet you do nothing to get them! Music gives you very favourable conditions, for it creates an atmosphere highly conducive to mental activity: like a strong wind, it fills your sails and drives your ship before it towards a new world, a divine world. Music is a powerful aid in making things come true.

Obviously, if you wish to create a bond with the divine world, you cannot do so by listening to just any kind of music. Unfortunately, the music of today is becoming more and more discordant and cacophonous: in fact it can hardly be called music, it is just a din. When I visited the World Fair in Osaka, Japan, I went to a concert of contemporary music. What a shattering experience: it was enough to drive you mad or make you sick! And as I listened, I realized that that kind of music destroys human beings because it saps and destroys the nervous system. One wonders if it has not been created by lunatics who want to drive the whole of humanity insane. Humanity is already a little mad thanks to all the negative work some people have done, and musicians are about to complete the good work!

Very few musicians have studied the true science of psychology, so very few are aware that sounds, words and, in fact, every kind of vibration has an effect on man. It is a question of physical laws. I have already spoken about the experiments of the well known physicist, Chladni. In one of these one spreads powder on a sheet of metal which is then caused to vibrate by means of a violin bow; the vibratory waves create lines of force which attract the vibrating particles (which we could call living points) and cause them to move towards those which are not vibrating, the dead points, thus creating geometrical figures. I have tried this experiment myself and I came to the conclusion that this is exactly what happens in human beings.

The sounds we hear produce geometrical figures within us which are real enough, even if we cannot see them; the effect of sound, the vibratory energy of the waves it creates, causes myriads of minute particles in us to arrange themselves into geometrical figures. This is why, when you listen to the cacophony that passes for music today, the pre-existent structure and harmony within you, the order that was established by the Creator, is disturbed and eventually shattered.

But just look at the young: this is the kind of thing they enjoy, music that stirs them up and makes them gesticulate and wiggle their bodies in a frenzy of excitement. The other music, the music of great composers like Mozart, Beethoven and Haydn, that's only for old fogies, apparently! Well, the trouble is that young people haven't understood the first thing about it: they don't know that the music they are so fond of arouses only the most superficial and insane impulses in them, and that some of it, in fact, has an extremely adverse effect on their behaviour and their sensibilities. They have never stopped to find out what this effect might be or where it is leading them. They don't want to know about that; all they want is to be 'with it' and have the music that pleases them here and now: they are not the least bit interested in knowing what the results will be in the future, or what mad things they will do simply because of an irrational state of mind induced by that music.

Now, I am not saying that you should never listen to anything but mystical music: masses, oratorios and requiems. Not at all! I often put on some folk music for you, especially Tyrolean music. It does you good to hear those young people singing and whistling and stamping their feet as they dance!

Besides, from the very earliest times, sages who knew and understood human nature and its needs, instituted holidays so that people could relax and enjoy themselves with music, dancing and plays. Even the Fathers of the Church introduced feast-days along the same lines as those of ancient Egypt and Greece. They would never have started such traditions if they had not known that this kind of relaxation corresponded to a fundamental need of human nature. There is something missing in people who are always serious and solemn, who never relax. They should listen to some Tyrolean music: it is so youthful and gay and spring-like! They are just nice young people, singing and dancing and enjoying the glories of nature all around them: the sun, he mountains, the sky and the flowers. And their joy is communicative: they make you feel as they do, that life is beautiful. Tyrolean songs give voice to the desire to be always youthful and happy and in love with nature, and they can communicate their energies to us and help us to do some really good work.

Music, therefore, is a powerful aid in achieving concrete results. This is why, when you are listening to music, instead of letting your mind wander aimlessly, you should fix it firmly on what you most need in order to further your evolution. If you need health, imagine, yourself to be the picture of health; imagine, that whatever you are doing, walking, talking or eating, you can feel health radiating from you and communicating itself to all those you meet. If you need intelligence and light for the mind, if you are always 'putting your foot in it' and making blunders, use music to help you imagine that you are learning and understanding, that light and wisdom are flooding into you, that you are even spreading them around and communicating them to others. Whatever it is you want to acquire: beauty, strength, will-power or perseverance, in whatever area you feel a lack, apply this method and one day, thanks to the influence of music, you will find that you have transformed many things in yourself.

8

THE MAGICAL POWER OF A GESTURE

I

Man, as you know, possesses not only a physical body, but several other, subtler bodies, and it is by means of these invisible bodies that he establishes contact with a host of invisible forces, intelligences and entities in the universe. These forces and intelligences often use man's gestures, movements and facial expressions as mediums through which to express themselves and, conversely, man can use gestures and physical postures as a means of communication with invisible forces and entities.

This question of man's physical gestures, therefore, is vast and complex and today I shall do no more than draw your attention to the immense importance of the motions and gestures we make every day, often quite unconsciously. We can divide our gestures into two main categories : harmonious and inharmonious. One sometimes hears people say, 'It's strange, but every time I find myself in the presence of So-and-so I feel ill at ease.' This feeling is often caused by that person's gestures; there may be other reasons, of course, but there is an endless variety of gestures and motions which make other people uncomfortable. It is important to learn to control your gestures, otherwise you lose any authority you may have and even make yourself ridiculous.

A gesture must correspond to an inner frame of mind. If you make harmonious gestures without having the corresponding feelings, they will not be totally ineffective, for all gestures have magic power, but they will not produce substantial results. The great Initiates and Masters are magi, white magicians, and this means that they know how to invoke the divine world and give it expression through their gestures, whereas black magicians use their gestures to exercise their evil powers.

Magic is the science of gestures, and this is why a disciple must be conscious of every movement and take care not to make useless or negative gestures as he is talking, walking or going about his business, for serious spiritual consequences follow on every gesture. Every gesture is a force which is active in the different worlds; every gesture corresponds to certain currents, colours and vibrations and has repercussions on innumerable creatures in space. Each of our gestures opens or closes certain doors in nature

and forms a bond linking us to a beneficial or to
an evil power. If we want to make progress on the
path of love, wisdom and truth, we must study
our gestures and see whether they express these
three virtues or not. The gymnastics that we do
every day, for instance, are a form of white magic ;
they restore harmony between ourselves and the
beneficial forces of nature and open spiritual
channels in us, making way for a communication
and exchange of forces from within and without
which has very beneficial effects on our health.

It is important to study our gestures ; some
of them are extremely potent and are capable of
putting us into direct contact with the forces and
entities of nature. But it is dangerous to know the
magical powers of gestures if one is not prepared
to use them for good. If you learn about such
things too soon in the belief that you are capable
of applying them without having purified yourself beforehand, you must be prepared to encoun-
ter great difficulties and even to be the victim of
accidents. This is why I shall give you quite brief
explanations to begin with, and mention only
some of the simplest gestures by way of example.

To begin with I must say something about
the gestures we make with our hands. The practice of punctuating one's speech with gestures is
very widespread. I am constantly horrified to see
how people make ceaseless confused motions

with their hands: nervously fingering an object, plucking at their hair or twisting a button on their clothes. When someone does this it is impossible to pay attention to what he is saying, and a few minutes of conversation leaves one feeling utterly exhausted. You must educate your hands and learn how to use them to calm your nerves. There are a lot of exercises one can do for this purpose: let me mention just a few of them.

For instance: stroke the back of the left hand very gently, barely touching it with the palm of the right hand. Or again: with the tips of the first three fingers of the right hand, stroke each of the fingers of your left hand in turn, beginning with the thumb.

Here is another: open your right hand, concentrate on the centre of the palm and then gradually, slowly and consciously, close your fingers, concentrating all your efforts on this movement, until you have completely closed your fist. Pause for a moment, concentrating all your strength in your fist, and then slowly relax your fingers and open your hand. This exercise should be done with great attention and gentleness. Once is enough; you will not become any stronger for doing it twenty times, but do it correctly every day.

The hands represent the will. You have to educate your hands and learn that each finger is an antenna which receives and transmits different kinds of currents and waves. Initiates know how to work with their hands and use them to capture the forces which abound in space and which enable them to heal and purify and to prepare themselves for their work.

During the course of the day, our hands accumulate a lot of impurities, and if we want them to do the work of sensitive antennae as perfectly as possible, we must wash them frequently. However, physical water is incapable of really cleansing one's hands so, it is a good practice to imagine that you are pouring a shower of spiritual water, a shower of light and pure colour over your hands. Wash and bathe your hands in this spiritual water for as long as possible at frequent intervals during the day.

Don't count on difficult or spectacular exercises. Understand once and for all that the secret of power lies in small, apparently insignificant gestures. Begin at the beginning, with the first basic exercises and do them regularly, with perseverance, not just every now and then, or without bothering to ensure that you have the right conditions: if you do that, of course they will have no effect.

Until you know what gestures to make with your hands, refrain from making any at all. When you are talking and explaining something, do so without gesticulating. Some people feel that without gestures their words would lose all their force and explain nothing, but this is false. It is increasingly obvious to those who have anything to do with films or the theatre, that the spectator can be deeply impressed even though an actor uses very few hand or body movements. When motion pictures first began, actors used wildly extravagant gestures, but nowadays the best actors try not to gesture, and the public is more impressed by a simple, restrained style. The most sensitive, intelligent and highly evolved people do not appreciate acting in the style of light comedy, with its unrestrained hand and body movements; they feel the need of a language from within, a language which does not need grandiloquent or melodramatic gestures, which uses nothing more than the subtle play of the face muscles and the expressions of the eyes. Try to gesture less, therefore, for every gesture represents a loss of energy, especially if it is clumsy or confused. When you make wild, nervous gestures they leave you feeling exhausted and demagnetized, whereas a few harmonious gestures magnetize you and restore balance and energy.

The gesture of shaking hands has a prominent role to play in everyday communications. In Europe, it is the custom to shake hands every time you meet someone or leave him — sometimes several times a day! But it is very rare to find someone who knows how to shake hands properly, so let me explain a few things about this. Some people offer you just half a hand, or a limp, dead hand, and instead of feeling any pleasure from the contact, one is left with the disagreeable impression of being drained and tired. Others, on the contrary, grip your hand with such vigour that you feel like crying out in pain — which is not much better!

When you shake hands, do so with love and sincerity; if you cannot do this, you would do better not to shake hands at all, for you will only be demagnetized and will demagnetize the other person too. And I must add that you should shake hands only once, not two or three times in a row. Why not? Because when you do it for the first time it is a mutual exchange, both of you give the other something, but when you repeat it you take back what you had given. The first handshake is an exchange of subtle elements; the second is an exchange of denser, more material elements.

It is possible to read a person's character from the way he shakes hands, for our hands have their language and they reveal everything about us. If you pay attention to what you are doing when you shake hands with someone, you can learn and understand a great deal about him. According to whether his hand is hot or cold, hard or soft, damp or dry, large or small, plump or bony, it will give you different indications. You can even learn how to talk to someone and how best to deal with him. Perhaps you are thinking that a handshake is not much to go on when it comes to learning about a person's character, but you are mistaken. If his hand is soft and flabby, you can tell that he is lazy; he always has innumerable schemes in mind but, as he lacks the will-power to carry them out he never achieves anything; he is a weak man who waits for others to achieve things for him. A firm hand shows that its owner is someone who likes work, order and difficult tasks; he is someone you can rely on. Indications such as these will help you to apply the method most appropriate to each case. Yet other indications can be seen in other characteristics: for instance, a hand can be alive, radiant and expressive or it can be inert, lifeless and expressionless. You are, perhaps, surprised that I say a hand can be alive or dead, and yet it is possible for hands to express even subtler shades of difference.

You can tell how long a friendship with somebody is going to last, for instance, simply from the impression you get from shaking his hand, for you will be able to get on well with people whose hands fit comfortably with yours: in this case you can be sure that your friendship will be sincere and lasting. When, on the contrary, your hands don't fit there can never be any true friendship between you, and you would avoid a great deal of distress if you realized, in advance, that you are not built to get on well together.

We must get to know all our gestures, and correct those which are neither useful nor harmonious. You will perhaps say that you cannot see yourself from the outside and that your friends will never enlighten you about something like that. That is true: it is more likely to be our enemies who render us that kind of service, but unfortunately we don't take advantage of them. Only those who are really wise know how to appreciate how useful their enemies can be!

In point of fact, though, no one else can ever tell you in detail what gestures you should make; each of you has to find them for himself. Some imitate the gestures of another, a well-known actor or statesman, for instance, even though they are often devoid of any spiritual sense — or even any common sense for that matter! Any gesture that is not the expression of a clear, well-defined thought, a loving sentiment and a noble, just will, is devoid of sense. You will never spontaneously adopt the proper attitude unless you are moved by love, wisdom and truth. Each feeling and each thought has its own particular expression, and they can only be translated into harmonious gestures if they flow from the soul and the spirit. Before all else, therefore, open your hearts to divine love and draw nearer to the sacred fire so as to become warmer and more vital; open your minds to the rays of the spiritual sun so as to find illumination and enlightenment in the light of God Himself, and, finally, bind your will to the will of the Supreme Being and from this close contact you will draw the energies you need to work creatively.

In fact I shall go further than that: each of our motions and gestures represents a sound in the invisible world, and, without realizing what he is doing, man sometimes makes a dreadful uproar. With his abrupt, turbulent, incoherent gestures he unleashes invisible whirlwinds which destroy everything in their path. With a harmonious gesture, on the contrary, he creates sounds as musical as the murmur of water bubbling from a hidden spring, the song of birds in the forest or the whispering of the breeze amongst the leaves; he perfumes the air around him with the fragrance of flowers. There are movements which restore peace, which confer as much strength as the sunrise on a fine spring morning, when the air is pure and filled with life-giving prana. Every movement of the angels in space is music such as man has never dreamed of!

I shall say nothing about all those hysterical

gesticulations which pass for dance and singing these days. Let me say, simply, that you must realize that every gesture is like a pebble thrown into the ocean of energies: it creates waves which inevitably end by coming back to where they started from. So if, at some point, you experience a painful backlash, you need not be too surprised: it is simply the consequence of a brutal gesture made in the past which has now come back to strike you. Each gesture releases a very subtle force which throws certain switches in nature, and it is up to you to know in advance what the result will be. This is why the science of gestures is so important. Our gestures have the power to lock or unlock the doors of our own prisons.

When the new teaching is recognized and established, educators will understand the tremendous importance of this question and study it for themselves. Personally, in my capacity as a pedagogue, I have already studied the question a great deal, and I have seen many things in schools and families which are very dangerous from an educational point of view. I have seen children whose nervous systems have been seriously disturbed simply because their mothers did not know what gestures to use in washing, feeding or caressing them. A human being is like a highly complex machine with a great many different switches on it : turning on one of the switches will produce a certain result, a different switch will produce a different result. You have to know how to touch the hands and feet and the body of your child if you want to educate or heal it.

But, I repeat, even the best gestures are devoid of power if they are not sincere. It is quite useless to adopt a charming attitude if it does not correspond to anything on a deeper level. Before you manifest anything on the outside you must be sure to have the corresponding thoughts and feelings within you.

It is true that even though someone may want to hide himself from others, his gestures always reveal something of his true nature and even of his past life. Just one example : if you see someone who is always rubbing his fingers as he talks, as though he were counting money, it is because he has been a cashier — or perhaps a usurer ! A few days ago a man came to see me : nothing about him betrayed anything about his present profession or his past life, and then suddenly, as we were talking, he closed his eyes and joined his hands in a gesture that immediately told me he had been a priest. And it was true. We sometimes have some tiny gesture that reveals the paths we have taken in life. So, don't delude yourself into thinking that you can completely dissimulate what you have done or are doing. If you have been an aristocrat, a tyrant or a secret agent, spying on everything and everyone, don't imagine that you can conceal the fact. Whatever you do, even the way you place your feet as you walk (if the toe or heel touches the ground first, for instance), reveals something of your true nature. For those who understand these signs, it is as clear as day.

Suppose a woman wants to attract the attention or esteem of an Initiate: she will go to see him and behave with the greatest possible sweetness and humility, without realizing that her manoeuvre will never work because the Initiate sees her for what she is. Certain of her body movements reveal that she has spent years pandering to her lowest passions and a desire to arouse sexual love in others — whom she then abandoned to their pain and torment. And if her object in going to see him was to satisfy her vanity by getting him to fall in love with her, she would be due for a bitter disappointment, for true Initiates are completely immune to such blandishments; they can only be touched by purity, simplicity, sincerity and kindness!

Countless men and women deliberately learn how to arouse sexual desire in others by means of certain face or body movements. It never occurs to them that the attraction will be short-lived and is bound to leave a residue of ashes and bitterness in their souls. Unfortunately, very few human beings know how to awaken others to the higher life of intelligence, beauty and constant regeneration, by touching the sublime being hidden in the depths of each human soul.

Body and facial movements constitute a clear, eloquent, vivid language for anyone who knows how to read them. They are like a letter that we are constantly writing for the benefit of the visible and invisible worlds. They are secret signs which put us in touch with the rational or irrational entities of nature. They are expressions of our minds and our hearts, and by means of them we have the power to create or destroy our future.

The difference between a white magus and a black magus is that the gestures and motions of a black magus destroy the peace of men's hearts, confuse their thoughts and drive their spirit far from the Fountainhead of life. Whereas the gestures of a white magus are full of purity, harmony, serenity and gentleness ; they are beautiful and sincere and they bring us life, illuminate our minds and release us from the chains that bind us to our lower nature. In the future there will be a school in which human beings will learn how to renew themselves and be reborn physically and morally, thanks to movements accompanied by music. Our Paneurythmics* is one such method.

I am fully aware that these few words about our gestures are a long way from having exhausted this vast and important subject. But I have spoken about it because I want you to think about it for yourselves. The main thing to remember is that every gesture is the expression of forces which come from very far away. All Initiates consider gestures as letters and signs by means of which they can read and interpret events and phenomena of the invisible world. Such phenomena take place in realms which cannot be perceived by our physical eyes and, after making their way through innumerable regions, they materialize in the physical world in the form of motions and gestures.

And now, may your souls blossom in the new life! May all your gestures be harmonious, and may your spirits become servants of the divine cause for the good of all mankind!

---

* The music and movements of the Paneurythmic dances were created by the Master Peter Deunov.

II

Our hands are like antennae, with the power to attract and absorb energies from the cosmic ocean in which we bathe, and if, in fact, we so rarely absorb these energies it is because our consciousness is occupied with other things or is simply asleep. Of course, we do receive energies from the cosmos whether we are conscious of the fact or not, but only physical, material energies, no different from those received by all other creatures, animals or plants. For, like plants, we have roots, and to the extent to which our roots are plunged into the soil we receive energies. But roots cannot receive celestial energies; only leaves and flowers can receive this kind of energy. The area below the solar plexus and diaphragm, the stomach, intestines and sexual organs, correspond to the roots, and the head (including the mouth, ears, nose and eyes) corresponds to the flowers and receives much subtler energies.

But let's talk about the hands, which are the

supreme instruments of magic. A magus is one who has learned to use his hands to receive and transmit energies, to channel them in whatever direction they are needed, and to amplify or attenuate them. Here, at the Bonfin, we greet each other several times a day with a gesture of the hand. You have no idea how significant and efficacious this gesture is — but only for those who are conscious of what they are doing. For others it is simply a convention. Of course, it does also depend on how you are when you make this gesture: if you are tired and discouraged, you will communicate this and cause others to feel tired and discouraged too. But if you are feeling on top of the world and ready to move heaven and earth, you will communicate this energy to others.

When an Initiate first opens his door in the morning, he raises his hand to greet the forces of nature: the trees, the sky, the sun, and so on. He salutes the new day and the whole of creation. Perhaps you are wondering what good that does him: it does him a great deal of good, for in this way a bond is formed between himself and the source of life. Yes, for nature answers him, you see. How often I have gone out into my garden in the morning to greet the Angels of the four elements; the Angels of earth, water, air and fire; and even the gnomes and sylphs, undines and salamanders. And I can see that this delights them, for they dance and sing for joy. And to the trees and the rocks and the wind, too, I send greetings. Try it for yourselves and you will see that something within you seems to find its balance and become more harmonious: many areas which are still obscure and hard to understand will become clearer and brighter simply because you have decided to salute living nature and all its creatures.

A true disciple of the Divine School knows how to send greetings to the luminous beings of both the visible and invisible worlds; every day he greets them and receives their greetings in return and, thanks to this practice, he can actually feel strength and light increasing in him.

As for the gesture of greeting that you address to other human beings, I repeat, it can convey extremely precious elements if you do it consciously, putting a lot of love into your glance as well as into your hand, and if you project that love for the benefit of the whole world. This gesture of greeting should be a true communion: potent, harmonious and vibrant with life.

Every single creature needs love. This is the only divine right that the Creator has given us: to love and be loved. The problem is to know how to love in such a way as to avoid misunderstandings and pain. But we must love! And it is by our efforts to make our love more perfect that we draw on that great Love that fills the universe. What makes you think that you have to hold a man or woman in your arms in order to love them? When you go for a walk with someone, when you talk to him or look at him, when you greet him — all that is love, and it is the subtlest, most spiritual, most etheric kind of love. You have all experienced this, haven't you? And you know how happy and full of light you felt. Then why don't you try to amplify it and make it last longer?

You must get rid of the idea that human beings were not meant for the most sublime forms of love. Do you think that angels and archangels don't love? Indeed they do! In fact their love is far more powerful, vast and intense than ours, and yet they have no need to behave like animals to manifest it. If you really want to manifest your love in a more perfect form, begin by learning to greet others consciously with an expression and a gesture of the hand overflowing with light and love. And when you are at home or out for a walk in the woods, what is to prevent you from raising your hand and telling all the invisible creatures of the universe of your love? Some of those creatures are simply extraordinary; they are far more powerful and more beautiful than human beings, and when you greet them they hear you and approach, whether you see them or not; their delight is to be with you and give you a share in their wealth.

When you give, you receive. As soon as you give something, someone else gives you something in exchange, for there is a constant circulation throughout nature. It is said that nature abhors a vacuum, and that is true: when a vacuum is created it is filled up at once. As soon as you empty your reservoir by pouring out your store of love and good wishes on every creature, Heaven immediately fills it up again with its blessings.

You do not know how powerful the hand can be. When the Hebrews went into battle, Moses raised his hands and the enemy was defeated; the forces flowing from his hands gave strength and courage to the soldiers. And when the battle lasted a long time and his arms tired, others came and held them up for him. If the hands can be used for war, therefore, why shouldn't we also use them to create love and harmony? If you see people fighting, raise your hand and they will throw down their arms and embrace. They will not feel like fighting any more when they receive the beneficial vibrations you are sending them.

If you learn how to raise your hand in order to capture forces and relay them to others, forces that cleanse, heal, restore balance and give life,

you will become a white magus. When you salute
someone with your raised hand you project rays,
forces; the five forces of five different colours.
You may say that you cannot see them, but put
your hand on your face and you will see their radi-
ancy, or put it on the nape of your neck and you
will feel their energy and warmth seeping into
you.

What wonders can be performed with the
hand! It is a magic instrument. And the things
human beings can do, today, with their hands, is
as nothing compared to what they will be able to
do in the future. Cosmic Intelligence has placed
the whole of man's future in his hand. Everything
that man possesses has been acquired thanks to
his hands. The hand is a living being with its own
brain, nervous system and stomach. Yes, indeed it
is! Just as the whole universe is reflected in the
different organs of our bodies, the organs of our
bodies are reflected in our hands. Our hands are
related to our bodies in exactly the same way as
our bodies are related to the universe. And this is
why they are so important and why we have to
learn to work with them.

9

BEAUTY

If there were no Cosmic Principle at work in the universe, if the Supreme Mother were not ever-present, working to preserve the harmony of forms, human beings would have become repulsively ugly. Considering the way they live, in a constant state of chaos, passion and conflict, how could they not have lost all their beauty?

One sometimes meets truly handsome men and women, but when one sees the waywardness and licentiousness of their thoughts and desires, one cannot help feeling that if absolute justice existed, they would be absolutely hideous to look at. This discrepancy between their inner and outer being is due to the fact that the inner life changes much more rapidly than external forms. The discrepancy, therefore, is between the past and the present. From one day to the next a human being can completely change his philosophy and his whole outlook on life, whereas his physical appearance will only change very gradually, for it is made of materials far more durable than the subtle matter of thought.

Picture someone, for instance, whose physical appearance is repugnant but who has embraced a divine philosophy : very gradually this philosophy seeps into his whole being and animates the matter of his physical body until, one fine day, that body becomes the exact replica of his inner life, the life of his soul and spirit : radiantly beautiful, truly divine. And the opposite can be true, too : a very beautiful person may lead a terribly degrading life, but his physical appearance will not change overnight. One day, however, it will change, and then it will reflect his inner degradation. It is difficult to judge by appearances, therefore. One is often misled because one relies on the visible form which is still an expression of the past. It is only a question of time, though : sooner or later the outer form ends by reflecting the inner life.

This means that every human being has an inner face which is not the same as the one we can all see, every day. This inner face is the face of the soul. Its features are not so clear-cut and unalterable as those of the physical face, in fact they are constantly changing because it is intimately affected and fashioned by one's psychic life, by one's every thought and feeling. At one moment it may be luminous, harmonious and subtly expressive, at others it may be sullen, deformed or completely blank. It is this inner countenance that we must model, carve, paint and illuminate tirelessly, every day, until it impregnates and fashions our physical face.

The face you have today was once the face of your soul. It is the net result of all the virtues and vices you have cultivated in the past, and even if you don't like it, there is not much you can do to change it now. So, instead of bothering about your physical face, you would do much better to take care of that other face which is the original, the inner model which has determined the form of your physical face. If you work consciously to improve the original, it is quite possible that your family and friends may not notice any great change, but the angels will, and they will bless your efforts. The physical face begins by resisting any attempt to modify it, but after a while its resistance gives way before the pressure of that other face, for the face of the soul is very powerful and it imposes its own features on the physical face. Even now, from time to time, one can snatch a glimpse of its beauty: when the soul radiates such light, kindness and nobility that its radiance expresses itself through the physical face, then we see, for one fleeting instant, the spiritual face, the face on high. Keep working at it patiently, and one day your two faces will blend into one.

But whatever a person's physical appearance may be, there is one aspect which cannot lie and which accurately reveals his deepest nature, and that is his fluidic emanations. If you are capable of perceiving these, whether he is good-looking or not you will not be misled. A person's emanations are an exact expression of his inner state, and if they are dingy, discordant and unwholesome it is because they reflect his dingy, discordant and unwholesome thoughts and feelings. One cannot really see a person's soul, but one can perceive his emanations. And if someone really and truly emanates purity and light you can be one hundred per cent sure that his soul is beautiful. Sometimes, in fact, a person's emanations are so powerful that, for all their subtleness, they become visible. There are people, for instance, who are physically ugly and deformed and then, for an instant, they undergo a metamorphosis. This is because, for that brief moment, their emanations have changed their form. There are three things to be taken into account, therefore: the form, the emanations which break through that form and which do not always correspond to it, and the spirit which produces these emanations. As it is impossible to know the spirit, and as forms are deceptive, the only sure way of knowing the truth about someone is through his emanations.

Behind the form, therefore, is something else

which we can know: the expression, the emanations of the inner being, the life which flows in him. And if we could go beyond this again, and glimpse his spirit which dwells in Heaven, we would see even greater beauty. But this beauty cannot even express itself through his emanations: it is so subtle that the physical body is incapable of manifesting it.

Actually, beauty, true beauty, cannot be explained at all. It is life, a life which streams forth, which emanates. Suppose, for example, you have a diamond; when the sun's rays fall on it you are dazzled by the brilliance of the colours before your eyes. Well, this is an image of true beauty: it can be compared to the light of the sun. And to the extent to which someone emanates beauty such as this, to that extent he comes close to true beauty. True beauty is not in forms; true beauty has no form. It exists on high, in a realm in which there are only currents, forces and radiances. When one succeeds in contemplating it, one is seized by such ravishment that one almost wishes for death. True beauty cannot really be found in the bodies or on the faces of men and women; it is in the world above. It is only from time to time, if a man or woman is in such close accord with the divine world that they allow some of its radiance to shine through them, that their faces can hint at that beauty.

Bear this always in mind: beauty is not in the form, it is in the radiance, the emanations. This is why you must not try to pounce on it to capture and devour it: it is not a form that can be seized. You must use beauty only to contemplate and marvel at; you must let its presence soak into you. If human beings use beauty to lure each other into the abyss, it is not the fault of beauty, it is they themselves who are not sufficiently pure; they kindle a fire within and then, because of all their impurities, it starts to smoke. Beauty should not cause the downfall of human beings; on the contrary it should lead them to God, elevate them to Heaven itself. I realize, of course, that this is a point of view which is so totally unknown that it may even seem grotesque. Most people behave as though beauty were something to be pawed, possessed, soiled and torn to shreds — like children who tear out the pages of a book once they have looked at the pictures!

Look at the thousands of lovely women who have been degraded and destroyed! Their lack of intelligence and enlightenment led to their being devoured by swine! Unfortunately, the prettiest girls are rarely very intelligent. And the same is true of men: the best-looking men are not often intelligent! The face of an intelligent man is usually ill-proportioned and asymmetric. When the trunk and branches of a tree are twisted

and misshapen, it shows that the tree has had to
overcome great difficulties in the course of its
growth, but it had the will to survive in spite of all
obstacles, and its desperate struggles are reflected
in the shape of its trunk and branches. With
human beings the same thing happens: the tor-
mented, deformed features of some of the
world's most remarkable people proves that they
have had to triumph in very difficult circum-
stances. The regrettable thing is, though, that
they have often developed their intellectual
capacities and their will-power to the detriment
of their moral qualities and the qualities of the
heart, and this is why their faces are deformed.
Beauty speaks more of moral than of intellectual
qualities. Yes, this is something you don't know:
people who are very good-looking are not always
very intelligent; in fact they are often ripe for the
plucking! And, indeed, this is what happens:
they are plucked and devoured by others who are
not so beautiful but who have learned how to
look after themselves!

Beauty has far more affinity with kindness
than with intelligence. Perhaps you will object:
'Oh, that's not true! I have known some really
gorgeous women, but they were she-devils!' Ah,
that is because you cannot see what is staring you
in the face. When you look at women like that you
can feel that there is something cruel, selfish and

treacherous behind the beauty of their features; that is not the kind of beauty I am talking about. Their whole attitude, even the way they hold themselves, shows that in their innermost being they are hideously cold and calculating and bent on getting their own way, and this can be sensed behind the outward appearance. Beauty has a certain simplicity to it, something entirely natural and uncontrived, almost naive; it is not treacherous and calculating, it is not particularly intelligent, but it is kind-hearted.

It takes a great deal of practice to be able to discern these shades of difference. They are something very subtle, as I have said, and it is not just a question of physical features or forms. Certain women are very beautiful, but one can sense that their astral bodies emanate terrible ambitions and lusts which will be the ruin of anyone who loves them. In a previous existence they worked to cultivate the qualities and virtues which are responsible for the beauty of their bodies or their faces; in this life they are not working in the same direction, but the physical body is slow to change, so, even though they are fast sinking into degradation, it still holds out and manifests something of its past glory. The 'lady of the manor' may be riddled with debts but she still lives in palatial splendour, for the fabric of her mansion is still in good repair! This is the physical body: the stones with which our house is built, and eventually even the stones crumble and rot. Only those who lead well-ordered, harmonious lives are working, whether they know it or not, to fashion their bodies and their faces in accordance with good.

Now, make up your minds to improve and perfect your attitude and your behaviour in respect to beauty; to consider it as the language of living Nature and a means by which to draw closer to the Lord. If you want to have some slight idea of what true, luminous, pure beauty is, take a crystal, a prism, and observe how light passes through it and becomes so beautiful that you could look at it for hours, enraptured by the colours you see. This is something I often do; it gives me such joy to contemplate the beauty of light, and I advise you to do so, too; you will gain a great deal from it. Of course, I know that some of you will say, 'I'm not ready for any of that. It's not for me...' but this is faulty reasoning. On the contrary, you should say, 'Even if I'm not made for that, even if I'm dreadfully weak, I've decided to nourish myself with beauty.' As long as you use your present state of destitution as the yardstick by which to determine what you can or cannot do, obviously, you will never do anything.

True beauty, therefore, is not on the physical plane, it is elsewhere. True, the earth is beautiful, with its plants, mountains, lakes and rivers. But I am bound to say that all the beauty of the earth pales in comparison with the beauty of the world above. Beauty is the expression of the highest perfection. It embraces intelligence, light, purity, music, colours and perfumes, and this is why, for me, beauty is always linked to the Godhead. The Godhead is beauty and, as I have already said so often, if God were not beautiful, if He were only wise, all-loving and all-powerful I would not love Him as much as I do. It is because He is beautiful that I love Him and want to be like Him.

Many people seek God because He is all-powerful, or because He is omniscient. I seek Him because He is beautiful. I have a weakness for beauty — which means that I have a weakness for perfection. So much the better: it is a very good thing to have such weaknesses! The only weakness you will never be blamed for, in fact the only weakness which is a glory, is a weakness for beauty: for divine beauty. I tell you frankly, I have seen a great many very lovely girls and I have also seen some very handsome men, but they have never really dazzled me because I have always looked for another kind of beauty, the beauty that is beyond the world of forms. That is what has always saved me: my love of beauty. And you, too, will be saved if you have the same love of beauty.

It is important to seek beauty, but not external beauty : you must seek inner beauty. If human beings took as much trouble to improve their inner looks as they take to try and improve their outward, physical looks, they would be living wonders. Unfortunately, the effects of all the care you give to your outward appearance does not last : you have to start all over again every day. Whereas, although it may take longer to make inward improvements you can be absolutely sure that they will last. Make up your minds, therefore, to dedicate at least a few moments every day to making yourself more beautiful. Why not go to a beauty salon ? Yes, but there are different kinds of beauty salons : in the morning, for instance, when you attend the sunrise, you are in a beauty salon ! When you contemplate the rising sun you are changing, improving something in your etheric, astral and mental bodies. The lakes and forests and all the lovely things of nature, are beauty salons. But the best beauty salon of all is the one within you, it is there that you must do this work ; every day you can make certain improvements and remedy certain inner imperfections by using the colours of the rainbow.

It is not only your face that will benefit from the work you do in your inner beauty salon, but your body as well. In fact, though, you would do better not to bother too much about your present physical body; concentrate rather on building a new body, the Body of Glory that we read about in Scripture. Every Initiate works at building this body out of the subtlest, purest, most divine elements he can find within himself. Every sublime moment of poetry, adoration or sacrifice offers him matter which he uses to build up this body just as he would model a statue. He knows that, one day, he will have to leave behind his mortal physical body, he cannot take it with him to the farthest bounds of space, so he concentrates on building his Body of Glory. And for this he uses all the materials that he finds at the height of his meditations and contemplations; all these sublime emotions serve to form that body, and one day it becomes so radiant and strong that it is even capable of raising his physical body and transporting it to distant places.

We must love and desire beauty. But beauty all by itself, beauty which is not at the service of something higher, can lead to the greatest possible misfortunes. How many men have committed suicide for the sake of a beautiful woman because her beauty aroused the jealousy and envy of others! Beauty must be at the service of an idea capable of elevating human beings, otherwise it is dangerous and destructive. Unfortunately, most pretty women use their beauty to get what they want: money, fame or pleasure. They are not interested in using it for the good of others, to help them to evolve, to ennoble them and transform them into poets. Beauty is a two-edged sword: it can do good but, equally, it can do evil. Women, therefore — and men too, for that matter — should be fully conscious of the use they make of their beauty and never forget that Heaven sees everything they do. It was Heaven that gave them this 'capital' and it is interested in seeing what use will be made of it. If it sees that someone uses his capital to satisfy his own selfish interests and appetites, not only will he lose his beauty in the future, but he will be punished, too.

And what I have said about beauty can be applied to all the gifts one has received: wealth, intelligence, fame, strength. They must never be used for one's own advantage; they must always be put at the service of a divine idea.

10

IDEALIZATION
AS A MEANS OF CREATION

It is very important that human beings should cultivate thoughts of a sacred nature for each other for, in this way, they help their brothers and sisters in their evolution and advance their own sanctification.

I know, of course, that this idea is diametrically opposed to the habit so deeply ingrained in most men and women of seeing only the worst side of people and events. If you can point out someone else's faults and failings you earn a reputation for perspicacity and intelligence. But don't forget that there is a law according to which the strengths and weaknesses we recognize in others are the reflection of our own strengths and weaknesses, and one who is forever criticizing others, therefore, is simply revealing his own shortcomings.

But we can leave that aspect of the question for the time being, for I want to talk to you about the consequences of the opposite attitude, which is the one I recommend: that of making the effort to see only the best points in other people. I know perfectly well that many will say that if you adopt such an illusory attitude you will be a victim of your own gullibility and will end by paying very dearly for it. 'After all,' they say; 'human nature is basically evil, even religion says so, so why fool yourself?' Well, to that I reply that you have not studied the question properly; you have only noticed what is evil in man, and it is quite true: it does exist. But man also has a soul and a spirit. True, no one can say that it is his soul and spirit that are most often in evidence, but they are there all the same, so it is always possible for them to manifest and express themselves if we give them the right conditions.

To make up one's mind once and for all that man is evil is not the way to prepare the favourable conditions which must be present if his divine nature is to manifest itself. Don't think that a sage does not see the bad side of people. He does: he sees it perfectly well; in fact he is very sharp-sighted in this respect, but he does not dwell on it because he knows that he can never help anyone by dwelling only on his weaknesses and vices. In fact, it only makes them worse.

A sage is keenly aware that men and women are sons and daughters of God, and he dwells on that truth; it is in the forefront of his mind in dealing with them. The effect of this attitude is to make his encounters with others creative, for he encourages the divine side of their nature and finds his own happiness in doing so. Believe me, this is the best way to deal with other people: try and find out what their qualities, virtues and talents are and concentrate on them. Sometimes these positive aspects are so well camouflaged that even the person concerned has never guessed that they are there. One has to get into the habit of looking into the depths of human beings instead of seeing only the superficial manifestations which are often very misleading.

It is all too easy to see people's faults. But to discover certain virtues even before they have been manifested, requires considerable science. Each one of you possesses divine qualities which are only waiting for the right moment to become visible, and that is what my work is: to seek out all those hidden qualities in you which have yet to show themselves. In this way my work affects both you and myself, and you, too, must learn to work in this way. So this is why you must cultivate sacred thoughts for others, for while you are doing that you will have to stop dwelling on details of their character which are not particularly glorious, and concentrate on the divine principle in them. Yes, why not cultivate sentiments of sacred love and awe for all that is divine, immortal and eternal in man? In this way you will be doing good work both for yourself and for others. Whereas by concentrating on their defects you are doing yourself an injury because you are feeding on filth and, at the same time, you are preventing them from evolving. Oh, what ignorance! People think they can help others to improve if they continually point out their weak points whereas, in reality, the effect is exactly the opposite.

Human beings are vicious and cruel and have every conceivable shortcoming: yes, all that is perfectly true, but it is no reason to spend your life seeing and talking about nothing but that. You have to keep your eyes open, I agree, but that is only half of your work. If you are always trying to belittle someone and showing that you have a very poor opinion of him, not only will he never show you the better side of himself which, after all, does exist, but he will also try to hurt you too. Whereas if you show somebody that you believe in him he will try not to disappoint you. Sometimes, in fact, you have to pretend to have a high opinion of someone, for this appeals to his self-respect, he tries to do better and, in this way, you help him to improve. Yes, this is the true science of education. It is no use thinking that you can improve people by constantly nagging them about their imperfections and treating them as though they were half-witted and incapable of doing anything right : if you do that they will not even try any more. Since you already have such a poor opinion of them why should they make an effort? And, in the end, they really do become incapable, because you have been working a kind of magic on them; they are hypnotized, sub-jugated and paralysed.

Unfortunately, there are a lot of parents who adopt this attitude because they think that, in this way, they will force their children to improve. They must understand, henceforth, that this is the worst possible method! If you want to get a child to make progress of any kind you must always encourage him, just as I encourage you. I believe in you and encourage you even when I know that the reality is none too wonderful, but my attitude helps you to make progress. You must never have a critical attitude towards people, because that simply paralyses them and, at the same time, they are driven to find some way of getting their own back later on. It is often far preferable to keep your opinions to yourself. This does not mean that you have to close your eyes and not even see that someone is robbing you or preparing to ruin you. You have to be able to see this, but you must not see only this; you should say to yourself, 'The poor wretch is like that now because he hasn't had time to develop properly, but if I concentrate on his spirit, on the divine in him, he will end by changing. ' In any case, this is how a Master works on his disciples and it is in this way that he hastens their evolution. And you, too : dedicate yourselves to this work. It is time that you awoke to the possibility of undertaking spiritual activities of this kind.

This is the activity — I can never repeat it too often — that parents must devote themselves to when their children are still very young : review in your mind all the qualities and virtues hidden in the soul and spirit of your child. Instead of weeping and wailing about his faults, and boxing his ears or whipping him in the hope of curing him of his mischief, concentrate on the divine spark in him. In this way, thanks to his parents who have nurtured and tended that spark, the child will grow up to do wonders. When your child is asleep, for instance, you can sit by his bed and, without waking him, stroke his face and talk to him about all the lovely qualities you hope to see in him as he grows up. In this way you can instill very precious elements into his subconscious. Years later, when these elements come to the surface of his mind, they will be a shield against all kinds of errors and dangers.

It goes without saying that if you don't like someone because he has, in some way, cheated or injured you, you will not find it easy to recognize the divine in him. On the other hand, if you love someone it is not difficult, no effort is needed; the problem only arises when it is someone you don't like. For such cases you need a method which you can apply consciously, secure in the knowledge that it will give good results. One thing which is very important in this question, is that you must not live exclusively on the level of your feelings and emotions; you have to use your reason and control yourself, and know that when you dwell constantly on a person's defects you are putting yourself onto his wavelength, you even attract his faults to yourself and, in the end, you will be even more unjust, dishonest and vicious than he is. You used to criticize him and now look at you: you are worse than he ever was! This is what I tell young people: 'Instead of loving and respecting your parents, you spend your time criticizing them, but be careful: you may do worse than that later on! It is still too soon to criticize them: simply show them that you are kinder, more intelligent and purer than they are; that's all. But don't criticize them because if you do you will simply awaken and attract the same faults to yourselves.'

I am well aware that you cannot fully accept what I am saying, at present. But in the future, everyone will learn to work mentally in this way;

when people think of their family and friends and acquaintances, they will think of them with light in their mind. No one will take pleasure, any more, in belittling or sullying others, on the contrary, they will only be happy when they are concentrating exclusively on the higher, divine nature of others.

Besides, when you talk about other peoples' qualities, even if you seem to exaggerate a little, in point of fact you are not really exaggerating: it just depends on what part of him you are talking about. Often, when you talk about someone, you are talking not about the real person, but about his intestines, his sexual organs, his belly or his feet (which may be very smelly and unwashed!). He himself, is a divinity. In Holy Scripture it says that we are all gods. And why shouldn't those gods manifest themselves? They are buried somewhere inside us, smothered by layers and layers of impurities; you may not be able to see them, but they are there! And these are the gods that we have to bring out into the open.

And now, let's look at the attitude men and women have towards the opposite sex. When I was still very young I cultivated the habit of seeing women as a manifestation of the Supreme Mother. I was well aware that most women did not manifest themselves altogether divinely, but I also saw that by adopting that attitude it was I who stood to gain. I wanted to see women as beautiful, considerate, loving, faithful and steadfast (which is not always the case — but never mind!), for in doing so it was I who thrived and blossomed. Everybody will tell me that I am hopelessly naive, that women are not like that; none of that is true. I know perfectly well that it is not true! But thanks to this untruth I discover truth, the truest truth! Because, in reality, women are like that on the higher level: in their higher nature they are glorious. And down here? Well, of course, the situation on the lower level is not so good — and this applies with equal truth to men.

The sad thing is that human beings seem to want to go down to the level of their cesspools to know each other. No, no! You have to climb up and get to know others at the highest peak of their being: it is quite different up there. But nobody wants to listen to what I say or to put this into practice, so they lose all their inspiration and become hopelessly prosaic. 'You've got to be realistic,' they say; 'It's idiotic to idealize men and women.' Yes, that may be true; but even if it is idiotic it is also very beautiful, whereas their reality is hideous. And, in that reality, without their realizing it, they are destroying their soul and spirit and laying waste the very roots of their existence.

Some will object that the advice I am giving you is very dangerous: 'If a man idealizes his wife, what will happen when he sees — as he must see, one day — that not a single woman on earth really matches up to what he has imagined? He is going to be bitterly disappointed!' Yes, that is true: he will be disappointed. If he does not know how to set about this work of idealization, he is bound to be disappointed and dreadfully disillusioned. But the idealization I am talking about is a work of creative magic and it in no way prevents one from seeing exactly what the person concerned is like.

When I say that I choose to look on women as divinities, that does not prevent me from knowing perfectly well whether it is true or false; why should I fool myself? And yet I still do this because, in this way, all my energies are directed upwards; everything becomes beautiful and expressive, and every woman I meet becomes a source of blessings, inspiration and new discoveries for me. I am neither a painter, nor a sculptor, nor a poet nor a musician, but I live perpetually in a beautiful world of colours, forms and sounds; I am constantly lost in wonder. And if someone says, 'What on earth do you find so wonderful? If only you knew the vices of all those people who give you so much joy!' I reply that I don't want to know. If they have vices, so be it, but their vices are theirs and the joy is mine. In any big city, for instance, there are all sorts of beautiful things to see, but there are also the sewers. Why would anyone want to visit the sewers? Confine your visits to the monuments, climb to the top of the Eiffel Tower — symbolically speaking. At least you can get a magnificent view from up there!

If some people who once had a tendency to idealize others have found that it had disastrous results for them, it is because they were not able to stay on that level; at some point they abandoned it and sank to the level of realization. If they had not lowered themselves, if they had not attempted to get a bit too close to the creature they idealized, they would still be happy and joyful. In the hands of the ignorant, therefore, idealization can be a real danger and the occasion of a serious fall. But in the hands of an Initiate it is the greatest possible source of blessings.

Idealization is magic; it is the best way to further your evolution but, I repeat, this is only the case if you continue on that course and resist the temptation to get closer, to get your hands on the person you idealize, to 'taste the sweets'! Otherwise you will be like the child who takes a watch to pieces to see what is inside and how it works: the result is that it does not work any more! Unfortunately, this is what most people do with the Lord's creatures: they

want to see what is inside — and inside they will
find the guts! Why be so keen on seeing that?

You have to idealize women — and men —
but you must never, never abandon that idealization; only in this way will you be completely safe.
If you abandon your stronghold that will be the
end of you: you are bound to be disappointed,
your friends will crow over you, saying, 'I told
you so!', and you will have to admit that they were
right. In point of fact, though, they were not
right: they were only right because you were weak
and ignorant. If you are strong and enlightened it
is you who will be right for all eternity!

Now, I must complete what I have been
saying by telling you that you can do this work of
idealization for yourself, too. Once you are fully
aware of all your faults and failings, you can
decide to imagine that you have reached perfection, that you possess every possible quality and
virtue. Once again, this is a magical method
which will accelerate your work of self-
perfection. As long as you always envisage
yourself only as you are at the moment, you
will mark time on the lower levels of evolution,
for that prosaic, mediocre self-image retards
your growth and prevents you from advancing.
Whereas if you form a sublime image of yourself and hold on to it in your mind, it will influence you by triggering other vibrations, other

impulses; you will feel impelled to attain that image and, in this way, you will make progress. Otherwise you will stagnate and never know reality.

You will say, 'But what reality? It is what I am now that is real!' No, that is where you are wrong: your present reality is not real, it is an illusion. The only true reality is that which is ideal, divine: this is the only reality. All the rest, all that we think of as reality is illusion, lies. You can only know reality if you idealize and divinize every single being, including yourself. This is what Hindus call Jnana-Yoga. Jnana-Yoga is simply a process of idealization: a disciple seeks to know himself because he wants to find the Self as it is on the highest level, with God Himself, and be able to say 'I am That', or, as Jesus put it, 'I and my Father are one.' True idealization is to find one's reality as it exists on another level, not down here. When we create this perfect, ideal portrait of ourselves, when we nurture it and define its contours more and more distinctly, it in turn sculptures and models and permeates us until we become a different being, better than we were before.

Once a human being has formed this divine picture of himself, it has a beneficial influence on other creatures wherever he goes, even on animals, plants and stones; on the whole of nature in fact, for rays, forces and vibrations flow from him, bringing order, balance and harmony to all around him.

How many people long to be loved, and do all in their power to achieve this! Unfortunately, what they do is usually purely external; it has never occurred to them that, if they want to endear themselves to others, they have to change inwardly. They have to modify their vibrations and make them much gentler, more peaceful and more harmonious, and this is only possible if one creates a divine image of oneself.

Now, just as there is a danger in idealizing others if you forget that it is an exercise, equally, there is a danger in idealizing yourself if you start deluding yourself that you have already attained perfection. If you think you are already perfect, other people will simply find you pretentious and utterly ridiculous; they won't be able to stand the sight of you! Your work is to elaborate and perfect the divine portrait of yourself as you are on high, but you must not imagine that you are already a divinity here, on earth, otherwise people will be justified in saying, 'Look at that silly creature; he thinks he's God Almighty! What an idiot!'

However great and glorious your inner activity may be, therefore, continue to behave with complete simplicity in all your dealings with others. Imagine that you are beautiful, luminous, radiant, that you are doing the will of God and that you have found yourself as you once were in God's presence in the distant past, and as you will be in the future! But never forget that all this has not yet come to pass on the physical plane.

All that splendour, all the wealth that is ours on high, must be brought down to earth and given concrete manifestation on the physical plane so as to achieve Heaven on earth. Heaven stands for all that is beautiful and most perfect in the world of ideas, and it has to be brought down to earth, that is to say, down into our own bodies, so that the fragile, mortal particles of our physical bodies be replaced by indestructible, crystalline, immortal particles. What a sublime, glorious task! And no one, or almost no one, thinks about it or does anything about it, and yet it is the only thing that is worth doing.

11

A LIVING MASTERPIECE

Everything in a man's life depends on the goal he aims for, on what he wants to achieve, in other words: on his ideal. An ideal is not something inert; on the contrary, it is alive and active and it produces definite results within the person who cherishes it: it cleanses, restores order, sculptures and harmonizes. All the elements of a man's life are fashioned, modelled and shaped in accordance with his ideal. If his ideal is not very exalted or noble, if it is mundane and material, everything he does, feels and thinks will bear its imprint, and he should not be surprised if he feels that something is missing in his life, if he is not happy.

The question is not to know whether your ideal is unrealistic and inaccessible: that is not what should concern you. The only thing that matters is that it be perfect, sublime, truly divine. Nor do you need to worry about how long it will take you to achieve it; that is not important.

A high ideal is a real, powerful, living being, capable of nourishing us and slaking our thirst for all eternity. It is because human beings have been unable to grasp this truth that they have always deprived themselves of the best. They choose an easy, readily accessible, material goal and, before long, they find themselves in a void. An ideal has magic powers: it is so intimately associated with us that we share the beneficial currents and particles it brings with it from whatever region it comes from. Since it is we who give it form and keep it constantly in our minds and hearts, we benefit continually from all that it contains, and this explains something that we may have already experienced occasionally: we suddenly become aware that new conditions are present in our lives and that it is our ideal that has prepared them for us. But if we want this to happen, we must be sure to keep our ideal constantly in mind, to love and nurture it constantly and, in spite of the tremendous gulf that separates us from it, cherish it in our heart and soul. Herein lies the highest wisdom and the greatest of all truths!

Henceforth you must learn to surpass and transcend yourselves, and overcome every obstacle for the sake of that ideal, knowing that it is a living being which already exists in the divine world and that, because of the bond between you, it will see to it that you triumph over all complications, misfortunes and adversities. The question is, do you have the faith, knowledge and determination necessary for the formation of an ideal such as this?

Those who do not know these great truths have to work with very brittle, fragile materials in very hazardous conditions. So, naturally, they suffer and bemoan their hard luck: but whose fault is it? They have never aimed very high, their only ambition was to acquire some mean, shoddy little satisfactions and, of course, they did not realize that they would not last, because they would be made of cheap materials. As you can see, the law of affinities, the law of like-to-like, is operative here, too: if you have a very ordinary ideal you will necessarily attract the cheapest, most ordinary, least durable materials. You must climb up to great heights to find the materials with which to form the organs of your body and brain; look for them always higher and higher, in Heaven, in the light, in immensity and in the spiritual depths of your own being. And you will only be capable of doing this if you choose the most exalted, most sublime ideal.

Most people imagine that their ideal will be fulfilled if they can practise the profession or activity of their choice. But then why are they always complaining that there is an emptiness within them, as though something were lacking? It is not logical: they have already achieved what they set their sights on. The fact is that they will always feel this lack if they do not adopt a high ideal, for only a high ideal can fill all the empty places in man: only a high ideal can slip into every little crack and crevice and bring fulfilment with it. I am not saying that you should not have a profession or a trade, that you should not be a scholar or an artist: not at all! What I am saying is that it is not your profession that will give you immortality, eternity and fulfilment. You have to work and earn your living, but it would be illusory to confine yourself to your work in the hope that it will bring you happiness, light, knowledge, power and absolute fulfilment, because it won't! That is impossible, because that is not where God has put these things. He has placed certain advantages for us in that kind of work, but not the absolute advantages we need for our soul and spirit. If we are seeking fulfilment we need something more than our profession.

The best solution, therefore, is this: have everything you need in life, but don't let that be your ideal. Your ideal should be so lofty that it is always beyond your reach. If this is the case then you are on the right path: you know that even thousands of years hence you will never be able to achieve your ideal but that does not matter. You cherish it, picture it to yourself, walk hand in hand with it and talk to it ; and it is your ideal that enables you to keep your balance, fills you with heavenly joy and transforms all evil into good. And, one day, your ideal will make a divinity of you.

The highest wisdom and the greatest secret of magic is to know in advance that you will never achieve your high ideal, but that by keeping it constantly present within you, you are achieving it in a way, for you are becoming constantly purer, brighter and more luminous. Your ideal will always be impracticable ; in fact I might almost say that there is no point in trying to realize it since you already benefit every day from all its wealth. In what way ? In all kinds of ways ! This may seem absurd, but it is precisely in that absurdity that you gain a great deal. Anyone who fails to understand this will never get to the essential core of the question.

Many people would say, 'That's all very well, but I know myself : I'm so ignorant and weak, I'll never manage it.' And there you have an example of how people give in — simply because they haven't understood. Man has lost faith in his own divine nature ; he has forgotten that he is a son of God and that buried deep in his heart is a divine spark which he must fan into flame by his own hard work. It is high time that men accepted and acquired a deeper understanding of this philosophy which teaches that we are all the heirs of our Heavenly Father, and that it is up to us to make use of all His knowledge, love, power and splendour which He has put at our disposal. That is how one approaches a high ideal: by modelling oneself on the Lord instead of on weakness, sickness and death. One models oneself on a truly divine ideal and, from its dwelling place in Heaven, that ideal smiles down at us, protects and consoles us and gives us everything we need. Whatever happens, never let go of this high ideal.

When a diver goes down to work on the sea bed he is connected by cables and air hoses to a boat on the surface, from which others keep a watch on him, and if he is in danger he can signal to them and they haul him up or send someone down to help him. Most people are like divers who are lost and alone on the sea bed with no one to come to their rescue: they are not connected to a high ideal, they are isolated and abandoned and exposed to the greatest possible dangers. Whereas those who have a high ideal are free to dive in and out of the water as they please. They can breathe freely and are always safe because their ideal bears them up and protects them and provides them with yet unknown particles. They are children of God, and they breathe a purer atmosphere.

You could find other comparisons and say,

for instance, that a high ideal is like a transformer which changes the voltage of an electric current. The fluidic atmosphere that surrounds us is alive with a dense web of unbelievably powerful waves and currents which can provoke psychic or even physical disorders in certain people; the very best way of protecting ourselves from these currents is to possess a high ideal which, like a transformer, reduces their intensity and makes them bearable. But how many people even consider it desirable to have a high ideal like this?

You cannot possibly imagine all the wonderful things a high ideal is capable of accomplishing in you. It is like a sculptor which models and fashions you, and it is here that we find the very highest level of art: in the painting, carving and modelling of oneself, in the writing of the book of Self. I have a great love of art and artists: art is a door opening onto Heaven itself, a path leading to the Godhead, but in spite of that I believe that there are higher levels of art. Artists create beauty, but it is beauty which remains outside their own beings, for they do not work on their own living matter.

One day I had a visit from a young sculptor who was, quite obviously, extremely proud of being a sculptor! His whole attitude expressed his arrogance and he spent his time criticizing everything. So I began to talk to him: 'You're a sculptor?' 'Yes.' 'I see. And do you know the laws of sculpture?' 'And how!' he said. 'Well', I replied; 'I don't believe you do.' 'Why not? What makes you say that? I've already created a great many works of art...' 'That is possible,' I said; 'But when I see your (I refrained from saying 'your ugly mug') your face, all twisted and deformed, I am obliged to observe that you know nothing of the laws of true sculpture for, if you knew them, you would have begun by applying them to yourself. It's no good trying to convince me that you're a sculptor. There's nothing about you that shows that you are.' Naturally, he was very surprised and rather put out, and he began to be a little less pleased with himself!

Yes, indeed; and a painter who never does anything to make the colours of his own aura more beautiful is no painter. A musician who never thinks of tuning his mind, heart and will, knows nothing about harmony. It is important to understand what true art really is. What could be lovelier than to be an artist in one's thoughts and feelings, in one's every gesture, word and glance? Every day we put our works of art on exhibition for the angels, and they come and see what we are doing. But then why do so many artists destroy their health and their whole lives in their eagerness to swagger about on a stage and be applauded by a lot of idiots, when there is an audience of angels there every day, waiting to admire their work?

He who uses the most beautiful colours and forms, and works meticulously, with precision and clarity, to perfect his own inner portrait, will never be one to complain that he is not appreciated or applauded by human beings: he knows, he has the inner conviction, that his real work is inside him, so he can never doubt or be discouraged. 'Yes, that may be,' you will say; 'But we can't see his work.' That is true for the moment, I agree; but as I have already said, there are hosts of invisible creatures in the world who come and contemplate and admire his exhibition. It is they who will be his critics, and if they like his paintings they will 'buy' them and his reputation will be assured on high! And if these entities decide to make him famous, one day, on earth too, nothing is easier for them. But this worldly acclaim must not be his goal: he must seek to satisfy and delight only his critics of the invisible world, asking every day for their opinion and advice.

In the future an artist will not be judged on his writings, paintings or sculpture; people will want to know the man himself so as to admire the poetry and music emanating from him and from his life. Everyone will want to live a life of poetry, and express music in his gestures, thoughts and

feelings; everyone will want to draw the features
of his own face, and carve the lines and contours
of his own being in God's image. Of course, it
takes a great deal of time, effort and work to create in this manner, but the question of time
should not deter us. The things that man creates
outside his own being never truly belong to him.
Since they are external and purely material they
are doomed to disappear one day, and when he
comes back to earth he will have to begin all over
again. Whereas a true painter, a true sculptor or
poet who works on his own inner self, will never
have to part from what he has created; he will
take it with him when he goes and bring it back
again when he comes back in a future life. The
work one accomplishes on oneself lasts for all
eternity.

I don't deny that many artists have left
immortal masterpieces which continue to inspire
the whole of mankind and contribute to its evolution, but in the light of Initiatic Science which has
revealed the goal of Creation to me, I know that
this is not enough: there are still higher degrees of
art. I have great admiration for cathedrals, sym-
phonies and statues, but the ideal thing to do is to
create all that beauty and splendour within oneself, to be a living painting, sculpture or poem,
living music or dance. You may think that nobody
else would benefit from masterpieces of that

kind, but you are wrong. The true Teachers of humanity who were their own works of art, have always set the world afire by the simple fact of their presence on earth, for all the colours and forms, all the music and poetry of the world could be seen and heard through them. A human being who becomes a living masterpiece, who writes the book of himself, does far more for mankind than all the libraries, museums and works of art in the world, for they are dead and he is alive!

The artist *par excellence* is he who takes his own flesh as material for his sculpture, his own face and body as a canvas on which to paint, his own thoughts and feelings as clay to be modelled. He wants all the beauty and harmony of creation to flow and be expressed through his being. An artist such as this creates the art of the new culture which is dawning in the world.

Beauty is something living, its source is hidden in the depths of every being, but it gushes to the surface of his body, bathing his skin and spilling out in the expression of his eyes, in his smile and even in his voice. Only a man's luminous thoughts and pure, disinterested love are capable of creating this sort of beauty. And when they do, nothing can stop the flowers and fruit which are blossoming and ripening in the garden of his soul from spreading their perfume, little by little, all about him.

12

BUILDING THE TEMPLE

Jesus said, 'You are temples of the living God.' Yes, when a human being strengthens his will, purifies his heart and allows light to flood his mind, when he expands his soul and sanctifies his spirit, he becomes a genuine temple: even his physical body is a temple, and he is entitled to call on the Lord to come and dwell in him.

Innumerable man-made churches and temples exist all over the world, and there is a reason for this. As long as human beings are not sufficiently evolved to understand the essential truths, religion has to be presented to them in material, tangible ways. But as soon as they manage to awaken and develop certain spiritual centres — those that Hindu philosophy terms Chakras — they attain a heightened understanding of reality and begin to abandon external forms because they find them far less vivid, intense and potent than their own inner experience.

To be sure, thanks to the fervour of all those

who built them and have prayed within their walls
for hundreds of years, the churches and temples
of the world are impregnated with an element of
the sacred. But even the most beautiful basilicas,
even the most glorious cathedrals cannot compare to a human body which has been purified
and sanctified until it has become a living temple.
It is when man himself is a temple, and when he
prays in that temple, that the Lord hears him and
answers his prayer.

Unfortunately, most human beings do not
take care of their temple; they continually
damage and misuse it by all kinds of irrational
behaviour. When they do this their body is no
longer a temple; it is a hovel, a filthy shack reek-
ing with the stench of animals, like the Temple of
Jerusalem when it was filled with the sheep, goats,
cattle and fowls which merchants had brought to
sell there. Nobody got indignant about that; they
considered it quite normal, but Jesus made a whip
of cords and drove out the merchants, saying, 'It is
written, "My house shall be a house of prayer, but
you made it a den of thieves".'

So don't behave like those merchants and
turn your temple into a butcher's yard, for it
will certainly not be the Lord who will come
and dwell in such a place; instead you will be
plagued by swarms of inferior, undesirable beings
which relish filth and feed on impurities.

But human beings are very ignorant. They don't know that the vulgar, animal lives they lead disrupt the vibrations of the particles and atoms of their bodies, and that the ensuing chaos acts as a magnet for all the impurities in their vicinity, so that they become like so many rubbish dumps! Then, naturally, as these impure materials are not radiant, light and subtle, they begin to ferment and decompose and cause various psychic and physical ailments; but people still do not understand: they see no connection between the way they live and their state of health. And yet it is so simple.

As I have often said, one can learn a great deal by watching insects. For instance, you must often have noticed that if you leave remnants of food lying about, it is not long before some insects find it. What kind of instinct, what kind of divining rod have they got which tells them how to find food so quickly, even at a great distance? And then, if you clean up the remnants the insects disappear again.

This law holds true on the psychic plane also. Here, too, there are all kinds of vermin which can smell impurities from afar and come rushing to feed off them. Everything that exists, on every plane of existence, is nourishment for some other form of existence. Evil, noxious creatures of darkness need to eat, and so do the heavenly crea-

tures of light. In fact, as I have explained in one of
my lectures, even God eats! Yes, don't be so horrified. Man eats, so why shouldn't God? Indeed
God does eat, and it is the Seraphim who nourish
Him with their emanations, that is, with matter
that is so pure, refined, and precious that it is
difficult for us even to imagine it.

Bear this in mind, then: as soon as you have
any rotten, mouldy elements lying about inside
you, there will always be entities from the invisible world who will rush to regale themselves on it.

There are so many people around us who are
perpetually worried, anxious and unhappy. This
shows that they are incapable of ensuring the
presence of the Lord within them, that presence
which would give them light and peace. And why
are they incapable? They should ask themselves
that question! The answer is that they have
introduced so many impurities into their bodies
and opened their doors to so many kinds of infernal creatures, that neither God nor His angels can
possibly dwell in them. But it seems that it has
never occurred to them that this is the reason. For,
until someone has become absolutely pure, it is
certainly not the Lord Himself who will dwell in
him, but He sometimes sends one or more
representatives, angels or geniuses. So if you find
yourself in the cold and the dark because you
have forgotten to purify your body, you can draw

your conclusions and admit that it is your own fault: 'That's true: I've done everything I could to get myself into this mess: I've invited entities of darkness into myself and now Heaven has abandoned me.' That is the truth, and you have to admit it!

So you must remember to purify yourself every single day, and throw away any black thoughts and feelings, and replace them by other pure, subtle, luminous ones. In this way you will be building your own temple. The temple that we call the Body of Glory, the Body of Light or Body of Christ.* I'm sure you remember the scene in the Gospels in which Jesus went up onto Mount Thabor and there, his disciples saw him transfigured, surrounded by a halo of blinding light, with Moses and Elijah on either side of him. What the disciples witnessed was Jesus' Body of Glory which had, as it were, taken over his physical body and set it ablaze with light. Each one of us has his Body of Glory within him in the form of a tiny atom, and we must all nurture this body and foster its growth by drawing the purest and most luminous particles from the atmosphere.

Jesus loved God and took Him as his model, and for this reason a multitude of heavenly beings

---

* See 'The Body of Glory' in *Christmas and Easter in the Initiatic Tradition,* Izvor Collection 209A.

and forces assisted him in his task of transforming matter. His ideal was to be like his Heavenly Father; he told us this himself: 'Therefore you shall be perfect, just as your Father in Heaven is perfect'. So he invoked all the divine Hierarchies and, while he devoted himself to loving and contemplating his Father and communing with Him, these divine entities came and sanctified his whole being and replaced the particles of his body by divine, luminous particles.

It was not Jesus himself who had to replace each individual cell or particle of his body: no human being is capable of doing that. There are other entities who know how to modify the structure of matter, and all we need to do is to invite them to come and do their work in us: we do our part by inviting them and then they do the rest. What does a farmer do? He sows the seed: that is half the work, and the other half is done by the sun and rain and the countless entities who dwell in the air, the water and the earth, and who tend and nurture the seed. The farmer has nothing to do with that part of the work: it is not his business. His job is to sow the seed. And an Initiate is like a farmer: he sows the seed, sets certain processes in motion, and then Nature and the powers of the cosmos do the rest.

We all have the duty, the obligation, to sanctify and consecrate our body as a temple of God, so that only luminous spirits shall come and dwell in it, so that, one day, the Holy Spirit Himself shall descend to dwell in it. When this happens, nothing more will be lacking to us : we shall possess all knowledge and powers, we shall live in a constant state of wonder and ecstasy, because the perfect temple of our body will vibrate in unison with that one, immense Temple of the universe. It is by means of our bodies that we shall, one day, be in communication with the entire cosmos.

The Lord is everywhere in nature. Nature is His dwelling place and His Temple. When we work at the construction of our own temple we are in communion with all the countless temples in the universe. We begin to have a share in universal life, to live in cosmic consciousness.

POSTFACE

I should like to conclude this little book with a few observations which are of prime importance for the future of art and even for the future of mankind.

When I see what is going on in the world — and since I am living in this world I can hardly avoid seeing what goes on — it becomes obvious to me that men are in the process of losing something essential. Many signs point to this: men and women no longer know what to believe or in what direction they should be going, and in spite of all their culture and science, in spite of so much progress in every possible area, they are more and more troubled and unsure of themselves. In my opinion (and since everybody proclaims his opinion, why shouldn't I tell you mine?) this is because they have no true philosophical system to refer to.

As each person is free to invent or believe whatever he pleases, we now have an extraordi-

nary variety of weird and wonderful opinions and
theories to choose from, but there is no one system
upon which everyone can rely. Or rather, there are
still a few surviving spiritual and moral traditions,
but the majority has ceased to believe in them;
instead they allow themselves to be influenced by
all that is deformed, perverse and obscure. Human
beings no longer adhere to that which is sensible,
ordered and harmonious: they are fed up with
that; they are clamouring for change — and are
ready to go to any lengths to get it!

Unfortunately, this tendency is most appar-
ent in art. Why are painters, sculptors, musicians,
poets and film-makers all so bent on portraying
ugliness, deformity and chaos? All possible
sources of inspiration have been drained dry,
apparently, so they have nothing else to do. They
are not capable of doing what artists in the past
did, and looking for inspiration on high, of perceiving and expressing celestial colours, forms
and melodies. So they take the downward path,
losing themselves in subterranean passages and
plunging into the murky depths of the subconscious. And here they find prehistoric animals
which have long disappeared from the face of the
earth, but which still survive in the human soul in
the form of instincts, impulses and desires, and
poisonous plants whose vapours cloud and
embroil the human mind.

Some claim that they are looking for new forms. Well, there is absolutely no reason why artists should not seek new forms; on the contrary. But why do they always have to go further and further from the Source and look for them on the lowest levels? They have never benefited from the guidance of Initiates; they have no science and no philosophy. They give themselves up to their instinct, their creative impulse. To be sure, whatever direction you take, good or bad, luminous or obscure, it is always possible to create. New forms and an infinite variety of aspects can be found even if one does turn one's back on the Source, the spiritual Sun. But these forms will only contribute to the corruption of those who contemplate them. It is admirable to want to be a creator, but you must face up to the question of the value of what you create, otherwise you will never create anything but gargoyles! You have given birth to something? That is fine, but what can it do for others? What will it lead to? Nobody thinks of that.

People explain that they feel the need to express themselves, to get something out of their system. That is not particularly original! Everybody needs to get something out of their system in one way or another, but is it really necessary to put it all on exhibition? Forgive me for saying this, but everybody has to get something out of

their system two or three times a day, but they
don't put it on a platter and offer to let you smell
it! But when it comes to art, that is exactly what
certain creators do: they put their excrement
before the public and invite them to smell it, and
even to swallow it! You will probably say that I
am exaggerating. No, it is no exaggeration! When
artists receive instruction in Initiatic schools,
they will learn to follow the true path of creation,
and give us works of art which reflect Heaven,
and inspire and uplift human souls. Whereas,
now, how could one possibly find anything uplift-
ing in such hideousness?

In the past, many artists were adepts of
Initiatic schools, and were taught how to rise to
the higher realms in search of forms, colours and
harmonies. They meditated and contemplated
with the aim of finding heavenly inspiration, and
when their works expressed this inspiration,
those who gazed on or listened to them were
influenced to follow the same upward path. This
is why these works still influence us today, centuries later.

Nowadays, artists leave their academies
armed with bundles of diplomas but knowing
nothing about Initiatic laws, so they elaborate all
kinds of theories to explain that their art is the
vehicle of a philosophy, an abstruse idea which is
incomprehensible to the man in the street. This is

unacceptable: if you create a work of art, the whole world should be able to understand what it means. If your work of art is for you alone, then don't expose it to public view: what is the point of showing the public something it cannot possibly understand? Here too, in the field of art, humanity has taken the wrong turning: it has adopted forms of expression which are meaningless, and now no one even dares to say that, in most instances, contemporary art is an aberration. They all genuflect before it and intone a chorus of Amens!

A few years ago in England, a painter put a certain number of abstract paintings on show which were widely acclaimed by the critics. When his exhibition was at the height of its success, he revealed that, in fact, those abstracts had been painted by his cat! He had gone out and left his cat in the studio one day, and when he got back he found that it had had great fun getting its paws and tail coated with paint which it had then smeared onto some canvases and produced these abstract 'paintings'! Of course the critics were furious. They had made fools of themselves by going into raptures over paintings produced by a cat! Can you imagine anything more idiotic? If that is art, then any fool, even a babe in arms, can produce whatever he pleases and exhibit it.

And if you need proof, what about this little

incident : a man who prided himself on his collection of contemporary art was showing some
friends round his gallery one day when one of
them asked, in all innocence, whether they had
been done by his children. 'Can you imagine?'
he exclaimed in indignation; 'The ignorance and
stupidity of some people...' Well, instead of getting so indignant about it, perhaps he would have
done better to think about the implications of
that question. Would anyone ask such a question
about a painting by Leonardo da Vinci,
Michelangelo, Raphael, Botticelli, Durer, El
Greco, Velasquez, Van Gogh, Delacroix, Renoir,
etc.? And there are a host of other names one
could mention: Giotto, Rembrandt, Titian,
Breughel, Poussin, Rubens, Turner, Holbein,
Cranach, Fragonard, Boucher, Manet, Monet,
Degas, Cezanne, and more besides. No, when you
see paintings by those artists you know at once
that they are the work of men of genius. So when
someone asks if a painting has been done by a
child, there must be a valid reason for the question.

The truth is that if you are an artist you must
accomplish something that no one else can
accomplish, something so beautiful and edifying
that it propels hearts and souls upwards on the
path of perfection, towards the Lord. This is how
Initiates understand the mission of art : to lead

human beings to Heaven, not to Hell, discord and disorder. Anyone can present horrors to the public in the form of music, drawings or films, but to do so is a crime against humanity because, in the long run, these so-called works of art influence mentalities. And if we see so many people becoming unhinged nowadays, it is because they are imbibing more and more disorder and ugliness from their environment. Whatever one sees and hears influences the nervous system, and when one sees nothing but disorder, disorder necessarily enters into one; whereas when one contemplates beauty and harmony one becomes beautiful and harmonious — it is a law of magic.

The development that has been taking place in the realm of art within the last few years is contrary to nature, and it goes by the name of 'abstract' painting and 'concrete' music! Take the case of painting: I am not opposed to abstractions, but is it really necessary to represent mangled and disjointed human beings and incoherent landscapes? There is no underlying structure, lines go in all directions, colours are thrown on at random, nothing is recognizable for what it is and the whole thing seems to be a return to chaos. And yet, doesn't life show us enough examples of how things should be? Suppose you are preparing to build a house: what are the first things you see? Untidy heaps of planks, bricks, cement, steel rods, sand and so on. Little by little, the foundations and then the walls begin to take shape, and one fine day, all those messy piles of materials have disappeared and we see a pretty little house, with painted shutters, curtains and flower boxes at every window. It started in chaos but the finished work is a thing of beauty. Or take the example of someone who is preparing a special gourmet dish: to begin with, her kitchen table is cluttered up with all the raw ingredients and none of it looks very appetizing. But when she finally takes the dish out of the oven, puts a few finishing touches to it and lays it before her guests, it has become a work of art! And, finally, take a human being: to begin with he is no more than a tiny drop of liquid but, little by little, things take shape and, one fine day, a beautiful baby is born!

This, then, is the natural course of events as we see it in nature: out of chaos come order, beauty and perfection. But men are moving in exactly the opposite direction today, especially in the area of art. One stands before a painting and wonders what it is supposed to be: a man? A horse? A boat? There is no more differentiation any more! The Intelligence of Nature, on the contrary, works towards increasing differentiation: a single cell splits into two, and a few months later a human being, with all the rich complexity of his different organs appears. Should we now go the other way and end by regressing to the unicellular? No! This would be to degenerate. And yet certain artists and art critics who are neither knowledgeable nor enlightened are doing their best to lead us to this regression, whereas the true goal of art must be to bring a work to a state of perfection and completion.

Nature is ceaselessly at work, completing what she has already started: one day, human beings, animals, flowers, crystals and so on will all be brought to completion — and in the meantime, the high priests of poetry, painting and music are trying to lead us back into chaos! Words strung together without rhyme or reason, in which everyone finds whatever meaning he wants; bizarre noises which pass for music! And in painting and sculpture, dissymmetrical, deformed bodies with disproportionately long or lumpy members! And all this is very harmful even from the point of view of the magic it works on us, for the human beings who read, look at and listen to these 'works of art' are being led backwards, to the darkest and most obscure eras of the earth's history.

I sometimes turn on the television because I am curious to see what is going on — and what do I see? As often as not I see a bunch of hairy individuals shrieking and gesticulating and looking more like animals than human beings. These, I am told, are musicians, and they are giving a concert! What a hideous sight, and what indescribable cacophony! And yet their audience is enchanted; in transports of delight, young men and girls are jumping up and down, wiggling and writhing and applauding wildly. When I look at all that I cannot help but feel sad. 'Dear Lord', I think; 'There's no understanding human nature! What has happened in men's souls to estrange them so completely from beauty? How can barbarians like that kindle such enthusiasm?' I am not so severe or strait-laced as to condemn exuberant young people who are bursting to express their surplus vitality and joy. But in scenes like that there is not much joy, and their vitality is expressed in such uncouth, graceless movements. Wild animals! Yes, I can see them: the cages are wide open and wild animals are prowling amongst them to devour any good that still remains in them. And the onlookers are applauding enthusiastically!

When I see manifestations like this I almost despair of leading human beings towards anything beautiful and meaningful. There is nothing I can do but leave them to sink even further until they touch bottom. How can creatures like that understand the great laws of nature and creation? They have never done a stroke of work on themselves: they don't even know that there is any work to be done. The only thing they are capable of is letting their own wild beasts out of their cages, that is all; and they call that freedom. Oh, they are free indeed: free, independent and unbridled!

I have sometimes talked to young people about the modern music they are so fond of and I am often amazed at their reflections and their reasoning. It seems that all the music of previous centuries simply does not exist for them; the only thing they know are their 'idols' as they say. They are so ignorant that some of them have even asked me to give them a list of the great musicians they should know. Of course, the list is a long one: Mozart, Haydn, Handel, Beethoven, Vivaldi, Chopin, Liszt, Purcell, Schubert, Schumann, Gabrielli, Monteverdi, Lully, Gluck, Bach, Tchaikovsky, Verdi, Paganini, Berlioz, Dvorak, Mendelssohn and many, many more. There is no lack of great musicians!

The important thing is to listen to music that impregnates the soul with beauty and harmony. I can never repeat this often enough: modern popular music is extremely pernicious; it encourages disorder and a lack of balance in young people, throws their nervous system into paroxysms and incites them to violence. Under the influence of this music they become more and more excitable and aggressive, and one need not be surprised to find increasing numbers of delinquents throwing bombs and attacking all and sundry. People will soon be afraid to leave their houses!

Unfortunately, the masses always prefer those who, instead of leading them towards the highest summits, curry favour by debasing themselves and pandering to their lowest instincts. Writers, artists, film-makers — they are all ready and waiting to please the crowd. They may ruin their health and shorten their lives but that does not matter: they are impelled to do whatever is necessary to please the crowd because they need the adulation and applause; it is meat and drink to them. When those who have a mission to guide and edify the masses seek, instead, to pander to them, it is a sign that a civilization is nearing its end. Of course, one must please the masses, but not by giving them all that their lower nature clamours for: spectacles of debauchery, cruelty and horror. What has become of the era when a whole population turned out to see the plays of Aeschylus, Sophocles, Euripides and Aristophanes?

Artists are unaware of the role they should be playing in the transformation of mankind. They don't know how to use the powers God has entrusted to them in order to stimulate and kindle men's souls, so they simply waste them. They act and sing and paint, but not in order to help people to evolve; they only think of amusing them and pandering to their whims and fancies or of earning fame and riches for themselves. And so many of them have a tendency to portray the crudest, most repugnant aspects of reality in their work — as though we did not know all that quite well enough! What people most need in order to blossom and flourish is a fairy-tale world of beauty which shows them that it is possible to live in a climate of wonder and encourages them to find it for themselves and try to live in it every day, always. 'But that's an unreal world!' you will say. No, that is exactly what it is not: that 'unreality' is the only absolute reality. It is only in this reality that one begins to feel that one is truly weightless and transfused by light, that one comes alive; whereas the so-called realism of contemporary artists spells death; it clips our wings and we are nailed down, incapable of flight. Instead of elevating and liberating us, their reality, which is no more than the husks, the dross of true reality, drags us down and destroys us. True, their works represent one level of reality, but it is a mediocre, shoddy aspect of reality because it confines itself only to the physical plane. True reality must be sought on high, on the plane of the soul and spirit.

Some artists do attempt to free themselves from the cruel bonds of matter, I don't deny that; but their ignorance of the spiritual laws prevents them from floating free in the higher spheres. They don't know how to reach the heights of their own superconsciousness so as to contemplate and understand the harmonious pattern of cosmic life and, having contemplated it, to exploit all the resources of their art in interpreting it. No one can become a great artist if he does not do an enormous amount of work on himself, and if he does not learn the laws of the three worlds: physical, spiritual and divine.

This is why I say that the only true artists are the Initiates for, like Hermes Trismegistus whose name means 'the three times greatest', they possess this science of the three worlds in all its fullness: the physical world which corresponds to the form; the spiritual world which corresponds to the content, and the divine world which corresponds to the meaning. Most human beings are almost totally unaware of these truths: for them the physical world is the only real world, and they neglect any subtler realities. Whereas an Initiate or a great Master dwells constantly in the subtle world: he breathes, thinks, works, desires and creates in constant communication with this subtle world, the world of true life. Even if we cannot see this life with our eyes, it is real; in fact it is the very essence of reality. And what better proof of that than a dead body: when someone dies, all that remains is a lifeless corpse, and that is soon buried!

A Master, an Initiate, is one who, by his intense spiritual work, has so greatly developed, broadened, deepened, improved and embellished his own being, that he is constantly in communication with the harmonious, intelligent, perfect creatures of the heavenly realms. This is why he continues to learn and grow and enrich himself even further, whereas others remain on the level of animals because they have cut their ties with these sublime intelligences. A Master is one who knows that at the summit of the hierarchy there is a divine world peopled by angelic creatures of such splendour and glory that it is beyond all human imagining. And it is thanks to his close association with these beings that he sheds nothing but blessings all around him.

Yes, Initiates are the only true artists; all those so-called artists who follow their own 'inspiration' without suspecting where it comes from, are poisoners. Think how inconsequential human beings are: if anyone sold poisonous or unhealthy food in the market or at the grocer's shop, their customers would soon call in the police and the culprits would be punished by law. But in the intellectual or artistic 'market' everybody is free to feed the public on poisoned food and even excrements!

People accept that there are scientific laws — the laws of physics, chemistry, electricity and magnetism, for instance — which have to be known and obeyed. In the field of ethics, too, there are laws which one must obey under pain of being punished or despised and detested by others. Then why will no one acknowledge the existence of laws when it comes to art? Everyone is at liberty to create whatever and however he pleases. And I say, 'No'! Exactly the same laws, the same standards and the same essential requirements exist for the realm of art as for the realms of scientific or moral activity, and those who fail to respect these laws not only fail to be authentic creators, they are criminals as well.

The capacity to distinguish beauty from ugliness, what is useful from what is harmful, the true from the false, belongs only to those who have been instructed in that great and precious spiritual science without which mankind must continue to flounder, suffer and destroy itself.

There, in a few words, you have the description of a true artist. The possibility is before you to meditate your whole life long and to read my books so as to learn the most powerful and effective methods by which you can hasten the coming of the Kingdom of God on earth and become a benefactor of humanity. Blessed are they who understand me, and so much the worse for those who don't want to understand! They will disappear without a trace, because Cosmic Intelligence will no longer put up with ruffians who refuse to abide by the laws. We must attune and harmonize ourselves with Cosmic Intelligence by vibrating on the same wavelength and creating true beauty.

The Bonfin, Frejus, January 14, 1986

By the same author:

Izvor Collection

201 - Toward a Solar Civilization
It is not enough to be familiar with the astronomical theory of heliocentricity. Since the sun is the centre of our universe, we must learn to put it at the centre of all our preoccupations and activities.

202 - Man, Master of His Destiny
If human beings are to be masters of their own destiny, they must understand that the laws which govern their physical, psychic and spiritual life are akin to those which govern the universe.

203 - Education Begins Before Birth
Humanity will improve and be transformed only when people realize the true import of the act of conception. In this respect, men and women have a tremendous responsibility for which they need years of preparation.

204 - The Yoga of Nutrition
The way we eat is as important as what we eat. Through our thoughts and feelings, it is possible to extract from our food spiritual elements which can contribute to the full flowering of our being.

205 - Sexual Force or the Winged Dragon
How to master, domesticate and give direction to our sexual energy so as to soar to the highest spheres of the spirit.

206 - A Philosophy of Universality
We must learn to replace our restricted, self-centred point of view with one that is immensely broad and universal. If we do this we shall all benefit; not only materially but particularly on the level of consciousness.

207 - What is a Spiritual Master
A true spiritual Master is, first, one who is conscious of the essential truths written by cosmic intelligence into the great book of Nature. Secondly, he must have achieved complete mastery of the elements of his own being. Finally, all the knowledge and authority he has acquired must serve only to manifest the qualities and virtues of selfless love.

208 - Under the Dove, the Reign of Peace
Peace will finally reign in the world only when human beings work to establish peace within themselves, in their every thought, feeling and action.

209 - Christmas and Easter in the Initiatic Tradition
Human beings are an integral part of the cosmos and intimately concerned by the process of gestation and birth going on in nature. Christmas and Easter – rebirth and resurrection – are simply two ways of envisaging humanity's regeneration and entry into the spiritual life.

210 - The Tree of the Knowledge of Good and Evil
Methods, not explanations, are the only valid answers to the problem of evil. Evil is an inner and outer reality which confronts us every day, and we must learn to deal with it.

211 - Freedom, the Spirit Triumphant
A human being is a spirit, a spark sprung from within the Almighty. Once a person understands, sees and feels this truth, he will be free.

212 - Light is a Living Spirit
Light, the living matter of the universe, is protection, nourishment and an agency for knowledge for human beings. Above all, it is the only truly effective means of self-transformation.

213 - Man's Two Natures, Human and Divine
Man is that ambiguous creature that evolution has placed on the borderline between the animal world and the divine world. His nature is ambivalent, and it is this ambivalence that he must understand and overcome.

214 - Hope for the World: Spiritual Galvanoplasty
On every level of the universe, the masculine and feminine principles reproduce the activity of those two great cosmic principles known as the Heavenly Father and the Divine Mother of which every manifestation of nature and life are a reflection. Spiritual galvanoplasty is a way of applying the science of these two fundamental principles to one's inner life.

215 - The True Meaning of Christ's Teaching
Jesus incorporated into the Our Father – or Lord's Prayer – an ancient body of knowledge handed down by Tradition and which had existed long before his time. A vast universe is revealed to one who knows how to interpret each of the requests formulated in this prayer.

216 - The Living Book of Nature
Everything in nature is alive and it is up to us to learn how to establish a conscious relationship with creation so as to receive that life within ourselves.

217 - New Light on the Gospels
The Parables and other tales from the Gospels are here interpreted as situations and events applicable to our own inner life.

218 - The Symbolic Language of Geometrical Figures

Each geometrical figure – circle, triangle, pentagram, pyramid or cross – is seen as a structure fundamental to the organization of the macrocosm (the universe) and the microcosm (human beings).

219 - Man's Subtle Bodies and Centres

However highly developed our sense organs, their scope will never reach beyond the physical plane. To experience richer and subtler sensations, human beings must exercise the subtler organs and spiritual centres that they also possess: the aura, the solar plexus, the Hara centre, the Chakras, and so on.

220 - The Zodiac, Key to Man and to the Universe

Those who are conscious of being part of the universe feel the need to work inwardly in order to find within themselves the fullness of the cosmic order so perfectly symbolized by the Zodiac.

221 - True Alchemy or The Quest for Perfection

Instead of fighting our weaknesses and vices – we would inevitably be defeated – we must learn to make them work for us. We think it normal to harness the untamed forces of nature, so why be surprised when a Master, an initiate, speaks of harnessing the primitive forces within us? This is true spiritual alchemy.

222 - Man's Psychic Life: Elements and Structures

"Know thyself" How to interpret this precept carved over the entrance to the temple at Delphi? To know oneself is to be conscious of one's different bodies, from the denser to the most subtle, of the principles which animate these bodies, of the needs they induce in one, and of the state of consciousness which corresponds to each.

223 - Creation: Artistic and Spiritual

Everyone needs to create but true creation involves spiritual elements. Artists, like those who seek the spirit, have to reach beyond themselves in order to receive elements from the higher planes.

224 - The Powers of Thought

Thought is a power, an instrument given to us by God so that we may become creators like himself – creators in beauty and perfection. This means that we must be extremely watchful, constantly verifying that what we do with our thoughts is truly for our own good and that of the whole world. This is the one thing that matters.

225 - Harmony and Health
Illness is a result of some physical or psychic disorder. The best defence against illness, therefore, is harmony. Day and night we must take care to be attuned and in harmony with life as a whole, with the boundless life of the cosmos.

226 - The Book of Divine Magic
True, divine magic, consists in never using the faculties, knowledge, or powers one has acquired for one's own self-interest, but always and only for the establishment of God's kingdom on earth.

227 - Golden Rules for Everyday Life
Why spoil one's life by chasing after things that matter less than life itself? Those who learn to give priority to life, who protect and preserve it in all integrity, will find more and more that they obtain their desires. For it is this, an enlightened, luminous life that can give them everything.

228 - Looking into the Invisible
Meditation, dreams, visions, astral projection all give us access to the invisible world, but the quality of the revelations received depends on our efforts to elevate and refine our perceptions.

229 - The Path of Silence
In every spiritual teaching, practices such as meditation and prayer have only one purpose: to lessen the importance attributed to one's lower nature and give one's divine nature more and more scope for expression. Only in this way can a human being experience true silence.

230 - The Book of Revelations: A Commentary
If *Revelations* is a difficult book to interpret it is because we try to identify the people, places and events it describes instead of concentrating on the essence of its message: a description of the elements and processes of our spiritual life in relation to the life of the cosmos.

231 - The Seeds of Happiness
Happiness is like a talent which has to be cultivated. Those who want to possess happiness must go in search of the elements which will enable them to nourish it inwardly; elements which belong to the divine world.

232 - The Mysteries of Fire and Water
Our psychic life is fashioned every day by the forces we allow to enter us, the influences that impregnate us. What could be more poetic, more meaningful than water and fire and the different forms under which they appear?

233 - Youth: Creators of the Future

Youth is full of life, enthusiasms and aspirations of every kind. The great question is how to channel its extraordinary, overflowing effervescence of energies.

234 - Truth, Fruit of Wisdom and Love

We all abide by our own "truth", and it is in the name of their personal "truth" that human beings are continually in conflict. Only those who possess true love and true wisdom discover the same truth and speak the same language.

235 - In Spirit and in Truth

Since we live on earth we are obliged to give material form to our religious beliefs. Sacred places and objects, rites, prayers and ceremonies are expressions of those beliefs. It is important to understand that they are no more than expressions – expressions which are always more or less inadequate. They are not themselves the religion, for religion exists in spirit and in truth.

236 - Angels and Other Mysteries of the Tree of Life

God is like a pure current of electricity which can reach us only through a series of transformers. These transformers are the countless luminous beings which inhabit the heavens and which tradition calls the Angelic Hierarchies. It is through them that we receive divine life; through them that we are in contact with God.

237 - Cosmic Balance, the Secret of Polarity

Libra – the Scales – symbolizes cosmic balance, the equilibrium of the two opposite and complementary forces, the masculine and feminine principles, by means of which the universe came into being and continues to exist. The symbolism of Libra, expression of this twofold polarity, dominates the whole of creation.

By the same author
(translated from the French)

"Complete Works" Collection

Brochures:
New Presentation

Live Recordings on Tape

KC2510An — The Laws of Reincarnation
(Two audio cassettes)

(available in French only)

K 2001 Fr — La science de l'unité
K 2002 Fr — Le bonheur
K 2003 Fr — La vraie beauté
K 2004 Fr — L'éternel printemps
K 2005 Fr — La loi de l'enregistrement
K 2006 Fr — La science de l'éducation
K 2007 Fr — La prière
K 2008 Fr — L'esprit et la matière
K 2009 Fr — Le monde des archétypes
K 2010 Fr — L'importance de l'ambiance
K 2011 Fr — Le yoga de la nutrition
K 2012 Fr — L'aura
K 2013 Fr — Déterminisme et indéterminisme
K 2014 Fr — Les deux natures de l'être humain
K 2015 Fr — Prendre et donner
K 2016 Fr — La véritable vie spirituelle
K 2017 Fr — La mission de l'art
K 2018 Fr — Il faut laisser l'amour véritable se manifester
K 2019 Fr — Comment orienter la force sexuelle
K 2020 Fr — Un haut idéal pour la jeunesse
K 2021 Fr — La réincarnation - Preuves de la réincarnation
dans les Évangiles.
K 2022 Fr — La réincarnation - Rien ne se produit par hasard,
une intelligence préside à tout.
K 2023 Fr — La réincarnation - L'aura et la réincarnation.
K 2024 Fr — La loi de la responsabilité
K 2551 Fr — La réincarnation (coffret de 3 cassettes)
K 2552 Fr — Introduction à l'astrologie initiatique
(coffret de 3 cassettes)
K 2553 Fr — La méditation (coffret de 3 cassettes)

World Wide - Editor-Distributor
Editions PROSVETA S.A. - B.P. 12 - F - 83601 Fréjus Cedex (France)
Tel. (00 33) 04 94 40 82 41 - Fax (00 33) 04 94 40 80 05
Web: **www.prosveta.com**
E-mail: **international@prosveta.com**

Distributors

AUSTRALIA
SURYOMA LTD
P.O. Box 798 – Brookvale – N.S.W. 2100
Tel. / Fax: (61) 2 9984 8500 – E-mail: suryoma@csi.com

AUSTRIA
HARMONIEQUELL VERSAND – A-5302 Henndorf, Hof 37
Tel. / Fax: (43) 6214 7413 – E-mail: info@prosveta.at

BELGIUM
PROSVETA BENELUX – Liersesteenweg 154 B-2547 Lint
Tel.: (32) 3/455 41 75 – Fax: 3/454 24 25
N.V. MAKLU Somerssstraat 13-15 – B-2000 Antwerpen
Tel.: (32) 3/321 29 00 – E-mail: prosveta@skynet.be
VANDER S.A. – Av. des Volontaires 321 – B-1150 Bruxelles
Tel.: (32) 27 62 98 04 – Fax: 27 62 06 62

BRAZIL
NOBEL SA – Rua da Balsa, 559 – CEP 02910 - São Paulo, SP

BULGARIA
SVETOGLED – Bd Saborny 16 A, appt 11 – 9000 Varna
E-mail: svetgled@revolta.com

CANADA
PROSVETA Inc. – 3950, Albert Mines – North Hatley, QC J0B 2C0
Tel.: (1) 819 564-8212 – Fax: (1) 819 564-1823
In Canada, call toll free: 1-800-854-8212
E-mail: prosveta@prosveta-canada.com — www.prosveta-canada.com

COLUMBIA
PROSVETA – Avenida 46 no 19-14 (Palermo) – Santafé de Bogotá
Tel.: (57) 232-01-36 – Fax: (57) 633-58-03

CYPRUS
THE SOLAR CIVILISATION BOOKSHOP
73 D Kallipoleos Avenue - Lycavitos – P.O. Box 4947, 1355 – Nicosia
Tel.: 02 377503 and 09 680854

CZECH REPUBLIC
PROSVETA Tchèque – Ant. Sovy 18 – České Budejovice 370 05
Tel. / Fax: 0042038-53 00 227 – E-mail: prosveta@seznam.cz

GERMANY
PROSVETA Deutschland – Postfach 16 52 – 78616 Rottweil
Tel.: (49) 741 46551 – Fax: (49) 741 46552 – E-mail: Prosveta.de@t-online.de
EDIS GmbH, Mühlweg 2 – 82054 Sauerlach
Tel.: (49) 8104-6677-0 – Fax: (49) 8104-6677-99

GREAT BRITAIN & IRELAND
PROSVETA – The Doves Nest, Duddleswell Uckfield – East Sussex TN 22 3JJ
Tel.: (44) (01825) 712988 – Fax: (44) (01825) 713386
E-mail: prosveta@pavilion.co.uk

GREECE
PROSVETA – VAMVACAS INDUSTRIAL EQUIPEMENT
Moutsopoulou 103 – 18541 Piraeus
HAITI
B.P. 115 – Jacmel, Haiti (W.I.) – Tel. / Fax: (509) 288-3319
HOLLAND
STICHTING PROSVETA NEDERLAND
Zeestraat 50 – 2042 LC Zandvoort – E-mail: prosveta@worldonline.nl
HONG KONG
SWINDON BOOK CO LTD
246 Deck 2, Ocean Terminal – Harbour City – Tsimshatsui, Kowloon
ISRAEL
ÉDITIONS GALATAIA – 58 Bar-Kohva street – Tel Aviv
Tel.: 00 972 3 5286264 – Fax: 00 972 3 5286260
ITALY
PROSVETA Coop. – Casella Postale – 06060 Moiano (PG)
Tel. / Fax: (39) 075-8358498 – E-mail: prosveta@tin.it
LUXEMBOURG
PROSVETA BENELUX – Liersesteenweg 154 - B-2547 Lint
NORWAY
PROSVETA NORDEN – Postboks 5101 – 1503 Moss
Tel.: 69 26 51 40 – Fax: 69 25 06 76
E-mail: prosveta Norden – prosnor@online.no
PORTUGAL
PUBLICAÇÕES EUROPA-AMERICA Ltd
Est Lisboa-Sintra KM 14 – 2726 Mem Martins Codex
ROMANIA
ANTAR – Str. N. Constantinescu 10 – Bloc 16A - sc A - Apt. 9
Sector 1 – 71253 Bucarest
Tel.: (40) 1 679 52 48 – Tel. / Fax: (40) 1 231 37 19
RUSSIA
Neapolitensky – 40 Gorohovaya - Appt 1 – Saint-Petersbourg
Tel.: (70) 812 5327 184 / (70) 812 2726 876 – Fax: (70) 812 1582 363
SINGAPORE & MALAYSIA
AMERICASIA GLOBAL MARKETING – Clementi Central Post Office
P.O. Box 108 – Singapore 911204 – Tel.: (65) 892 0503 – Fax: (65) 95 199 198
E-mail: harvard1@mbox4.signet.com.sg
SPAIN
ASOCIACIÓN PROSVETA ESPAÑOLA – C/ Ausias March n° 23 Ático
SP-08010 Barcelona — Tel.: (34) (3) 412 31 85 – Fax: (34) (3) 302 13 72
SWITZERLAND
PROSVETA Société Coopérative – CH - 1808 Les Monts-de-Corsier
Tel.: (41) 21 921 92 18 – Fax: (41) 21 922 92 04
E-mail: prosveta@swissonline.ch
UNITED STATES
PROSVETA U.S.A. – P.O. Box 1176 – New Smyrna Beach, FL 32170-1176
Tel. / Fax: (904) 428-1465
E-mail: sales@prosveta-usa.com — www.prosveta-usa.com
VENEZUELA
BETTY MUNÕZ – Urbanización Los Corales – avenida Principal
Quinta La Guarapa – LA GUAÏRA – Municipio Vargas

Printed by
Imprimerie H.L.N.
Sherbrooke (Québec) Canada
in April 2000